After Lament

After Lament

Psalms for Learning to Trust Again

GLENN PEMBERTON

Abilene Christian University Press

AFTER LAMENT
Psalms for Learning to Trust Again

ACU
PRESS

Copyright 2014 by Glenn Pemberton

ISBN 978-0-89112-487-0

Printed in the United States of America

Cover design by Thinkpen Design, Inc.
Interior text design by Sandy Armstrong, Strong Design

For information contact:
Abilene Christian University Press
1626 Campus Court
Abilene, Texas 79601

1–877–816–4455
www.abilenechristianuniversitypress.com

14 15 16 17 18 19 / 8 7 6 5 4 3 2 1

For Dana

who has helped me learn

to trust God and live again

Table of Contents

Acknowledgements

I have many people to thank for the opportunity to bring this project to life, beginning with the hundreds of students who have discussed the psalms that come *After Lament* with me, challenging my ideas with their own insightful and creative observations. I am grateful to my home institution, Abilene Christian University, for the Faculty Renewal Leave in the spring semester of 2013 when I was able to write a first and second draft of this book. I am also indebted to the NCA colloquium of Hebrew Bible specialists at ACU for their vigorous discussion of this project that, among other contributions, significantly impacted my approach outlined in chapter three (Dr. Mark Hamilton, Dr. Jonathan Huddleston, Dr. Melinda Thompson, Dr. Rodney Ashlock, Dr. John Willis, and Dr. Kilnam Cha). I have also been blessed by the constant encouragement of my departmental chair, Dr. Rodney Ashlock.

I am indebted to my team of medical specialists for their efforts to relieve my pain and keep my mind sharp enough to teach and write: Dr. Robbie Cooksey, Dr. Corey Brown, Dr. Daniel Vaughan, Dr. Larry Norsworthy, Dr. Gary Heath, and Shona Preston, MSN, FNP. I still benefit from the presence of good friends who continue to walk alongside me on this journey: Curt and Deborah Niccum, Mollie and Wade Spaulding, Jeanine and Paul Varner, Larry Henderson, Robert Oglesby, Jr., and Lesa Breeding.

My research assistant for this project has been Joe Ross, a graduate of Oklahoma State University and a candidate at ACU for the Master of Arts in Theology. Joe's assistance has been vital to this project, helping chase down a myriad of details and reading drafts with a keen eye for smooth, readable prose. Thanks Joe—*rid'em Cowboys, go Orange and Black!*

I am able to write because God has brought my wife Dana into my life. For this project Dana prepared a place in our home where I could work comfortably—bookshelves, writing desk, and chairs with ottomans and pillows. She takes care of my needs at the expense of her own work so that I am able to spend my daily allotment of working hours in productive writing. The perfect travel agent and advocate for her husband. My trusted first reader and editor. I thank God for you.

Reading This Book

After Lament builds on my first work on the Psalms, *Hurting with God: Learning to Lament with the Psalms* (ACU Press, 2012). Ideally, the reader will benefit most from first reading *Hurting with God* before tackling *After Lament*. However, I have been aware at every turn of the page that many will read *After Lament* before or without ever consulting *Hurting with God*. So to the reader wondering if this text will be legible without the previous volume, the answer is yes.

As in the first volume my goal is to write engaging prose on the foundation of my academic study of the Psalms. Consequently, *After Lament* falls between the shelves of an academic treatise and popular Christian writing—a space that deserves the efforts of many more academically trained writers. One downside to such writing is the frustration of my academic colleagues for a lack of detail and scant reference to secondary literature. The other downside is an uncertainty by non-academics of how to go about reading the book; to be specific, should the reader look up and read every psalm or reference made in the study? My recommendation is that the first time through the book the reader should just read what is provided in *After Lament*; then, if a reader has reason to go back for further study (perhaps for teaching a Bible class), he or she may want to take the time to follow some of the Bible references.

I have been surprised to discover that no other volume in print focuses on the psalms that come after lament. (I am certain to find a dozen as soon as *After Lament* goes to press.) Consequently, I am unable to refer the reader to other volumes that focus solely on the subject. Instead, recommended readings in Appendix III refer to isolated chapters in introductions to the Psalms and commentaries. These references are provided for those who may be teaching about the psalms that come after lament or those beginning further research. My hope is that this brief study will spur further consideration of these psalms by both academics and pastors.

CHAPTER ONE

Lament Is
the ~~End~~ Beginning

The Book of Job tells the story of a man whose character exemplified the teachings of Proverbs. Not only does the narrator introduce Job as "blameless and upright; he feared God and shunned evil" (Job 1:1). God also boasts of Job's integrity when he speaks to the Satan: "There is no one on earth like him; he is blameless and upright, a man who fears God and shuns evil" (Job 1:8). Consequently, in the eyes of Job, his friends, and a good many readers of the book, it was precisely because of his goodness that Job was so incredibly wealthy, "the greatest man among all the people of the East" (Job 1:3).

1. Unthinkable Losses: Job

But then the unthinkable happened. Job lost it all: oxen and donkeys (1:13–15), sheep (1:16), camels (1:17), the servants tending to these possessions, and then his children—all ten in a single day and single event (1:18–19). Then, just for kicks, Job lost his health; afflicted with sores from head to toe, he sits on the ashes of yesterday's trash and scrapes himself with a broken potshard (2:7–8). At first, when he lost his children, Job responded to God with humble praise; he got up, tore his robe, and shaved his head as a sign of mourning, then fell to the ground and said, "the LORD gave and the LORD has taken away; may the name of the LORD be praised" (1:21). But when his physical suffering leapt off every descriptive pain scale, his praise turns to bitter lament and harsh accusation against God.

> Why is light given to one in misery,
>> and life to the bitter in soul,
> who long for death, but it does not come,
>> and dig for it more than for hidden treasures;
> who rejoice exceedingly,
>> and are glad when they find the grave? (Job 3:20–23)

> For the arrows of the Almighty are in me;
>> my spirit drinks their poison;
> the terrors of God are arrayed against me. (Job 6:4)

In Job's and his friends' theological worldview, the righteous are blessed and the wicked are punished—in proportion to a person's sin or righteousness. Thus, on the one hand, Job's friends are confident that Job must have secretly done horrific things to merit what God has brought down on him (for example, see Eliphaz's speech in Job 22). But on the other hand, Job knows that he has done nothing to deserve this degree of suffering (see his oath of innocence in Job 31). Consequently, his theological world is in the trash-heap with him. What he has always believed to be true about God and how God's world works has been shattered into a million little pieces. A fraud from the beginning, he just didn't know it.

In Job 3–37, Job's lament consists of approximately nineteen chapters that address God (about God) and his friends (about their words and behavior). Then, after Job's lament is over, the book concludes in four unexpected and paradoxical ways. First, God delivers two speeches hot enough to singe what hair might have grown back on Job's head (Job 38–41). Second, God declares that Job has spoken what is right about

God, not the friends (who held the party line in defense of God; 42:7). And God instructs the friends to ask Job to intercede for them with sacrifice and prayer (42:7–8). Third, the LORD restored Job's fortunes, blessing "the latter part of Job's life more than the former part" (42:12). Not only does the LORD double Job's possessions (42:10), but he fathers ten more children—seven sons and three daughters (42:13). Fourth, Job lives another one hundred forty years, long enough to see his grandchildren, great-grandchildren, and even his great-great-grandchildren (42:16–17).

When I teach classes on the Book of Job, I conclude with the question: "Does Job live happily ever after?" Then I sit back to watch the fireworks. Actually, the students' initial response to the question falls somewhere between bold settlement of issues and puzzlement. A few students go into temporary shutdown mode—they cannot or will not go where such a question may lead (or they have found a good movie on their iPads). At first and even second glance the writer seems to want us to believe that Job lived a storybook ending with great-great-grandchildren swaddled in his arms, great-grandchildren lending a hand with the immense herds, his senior citizen grandchildren enjoying their own high esteem as community leaders in the city gates, and his children—*his children.* . . . ? Ask Job how many children he has and the veneer of happy-ever-after begins to crack. How many, Job? Ten—seven sons and three magnificent daughters. Or does he answer, "Twenty," with the question evoking the names and faces of the first ten that the LORD killed and Job buried (1:18–19, 21; 2:3). God may double his possessions and give Job ten new children, but children are not replaceable parts. When does a parent no longer remember a buried child? How long does it take to stop grieving for what might have been—or the empty spaces at holiday gatherings?

Does Job live happily ever after or is the end of this story more complex? If anything could be worse than losing a child (or ten), it would have to be the realization that the same thing could happen all over again, and that I am powerless to stop it. Before, at the beginning of the book, Job believed that as long as he lived a blameless and upright life, and made sacrifices on behalf of his children *just in case* his children might have cursed God, then all would be well (1:4–5). He could sleep at night with confidence that there would be no midnight phone call or 2 a.m. knock on the door. Nothing would go wrong because that was the agreement he had with God, endlessly repeated in Proverbs:

> Treasures gained by wickedness do not profit,
> > *but righteousness delivers from death.* (Prov 10:2,
> > emphasis mine)
>
> What the wicked dread will come upon them,
> > but the desire of the righteous will be granted.
> When the tempest passes, the wicked are no more,
> > but the righteous are established forever. (Prov
> > 10:24–25)
>
> The house of the wicked is destroyed,
> > but the tent of the upright flourishes. (Prov 14:11)

But now, after the storm has passed by and his home was destroyed, for the next one hundred forty years Job has to live with the fact that it could happen all over again—today, tomorrow, or next week—whether he is righteous or unrighteous. His understanding of God and God's world has fundamentally changed. And not only might the next messenger from the herds bring bad news, there was nothing Job could do to prevent it. Nothing. No guarantees. Job's lament is past, but the story is far from over. Job and God have much work to do if their relationship is ever to be anything like it was before the test.

2. A Walk to Remember: Abraham and Isaac

Genesis 22 tells another of scripture's most heart-wrenching stories. After so many years waiting for the promised son, when he finally comes and brings laughter (Isaac = he laughs), and grows up in defiance of high infant and childhood mortality rates in the ancient Near

East, the LORD (without need of the Satan this time) devises a test. He tells Abraham to take his son, his only loved son (Ishmael seems not to count), and sacrifice Isaac as a burnt offering (Gen 22:1). God inexplicably sets aside his own future prohibitions against child/human sacrifice (Lev 18:21, 20:2–5), just as Abraham mysteriously bypasses his usual readiness to argue with God. This is the same Abraham who argued with God for the sake of Lot and his family, asserting that the Judge of the earth must do what is right (Gen 18:25). And this is the same man who was distressed over Sarah's plan to throw Hagar and Ishamael into the wilderness (Gen 21:11). But now Abraham obeys God without so much as whimper of defiance.

Early the next morning he loads up, leaves, and three days later looks up to see the place God has selected, Mount Moriah (22:2). He restrains his servants with words, telling them to stay with the donkeys "while I and the boy go over there. We will worship and then *we will* come back to you" (Gen 22:5, emphasis mine). So they divide what must be carried and "*the two of them* walk on together" (Gen 22:6b, emphasis mine). Abraham fends off Isaac's question about the need for an animal to sacrifice with the ambiguous line, "God himself will provide the lamb" (Gen 22:8). And then, once again, "*the two of them* walked on together" (Gen 22:8, emphasis mine).

What happens on the mountain is clearer than *how* it happens. The next thing we know is that old Abraham has bound the young, strong Isaac, and is on the verge of slitting his throat when God finally puts a stop to the absurdity (Gen 22:9–12). The rest of the story plays out more like the script we expect of this God. Abraham looks up, sees the ram caught up in the bushes, and swaps out the ram for the son. All's well that ends well.

Until we raise the question we asked about the end of Job's life: do Abraham and Isaac live happily ever after? Once saved on the verge of killing/or being killed on the order of Abraham's God, what happens next? A hymn of thanksgiving? Exuberant joy and praise? Notice the author's careful description: "Then Abraham returned to his servants, and they set off together for Beersheba" (22:19). Do you see what or *who* is missing? Repeatedly, on the way up the mountain the writer emphasized that father and son walked together every step of the way (Gen 22:5b, 6b, 8b). But now after seeing death in the eyes of his father and a last second reprieve, Isaac is not with his father. Abraham walks alone back to the servants, with some explaining to do to Sarah about where her son has gone—and why.

Just as something happened on the ash-heap with Job, something happened on Mount Moriah that cannot be dismissed as if it doesn't matter. "Abraham's God very nearly had me (Isaac) killed. My father (Abraham) was stopped at the last moment; but he was going to do it. He had me hog-tied and strapped down to an altar, with a knife in his hand ready to kill me. So you go ahead with your songs of thanksgiving and praise for a God who provides, but I have some issues to work through with a God who uses my life for a true/false question; not to mention issues with my father who goes along with this God." I imagine Abraham having similar thoughts about his God swirling in his head. Some Rabbinic tradition attributes the death of Sarah recorded in the next chapter (Gen 23) to the events on the mountain. When she heard what Abraham had done, how close Isaac came to death at the hands of her husband and her God, she died of shock.

3. Pleasant Words for God: Naomi and Ruth

In the book of Ruth a family faces famine with a life or death decision to stay or leave home. Elimelech, Naomi, and their sons Mahlon and Chilion decide to migrate to Moab (Ruth 1:1–2). Then, without explanation, the writer reports the death of Elimelech (1:3). Widowed, Naomi at least still has her two sons, for whom she acquires Moabite wives (1:4). Her action goes against Mosaic law (Deut 7:3–4; Exod 34:16), but just how is a widow to survive in a foreign land? But no sooner are they wed than the writer reports, again with no explanation, that both of her sons die (1:5). Inside ten years, Naomi has buried her husband and both sons. All she has left are two Moabite daughters-in-law hung around her neck and a life not working out according to the meaning of her name: Pleasant.

Most studies of the Book of Ruth focus on Ruth: her determination to stay with her mother-in-law (1:6–18), her risk-taking going out to glean in the fields (2:-23), and her forward action to push men in the story to do what they should have already done to help these widows (3:1–4:12). Here, however, I want to draw attention to Naomi (Pleasant) and what she says about God and herself. First, in her efforts to persuade both daughters-in-law to return to their own homes, she seeks the LORD's blessing for them (1:8–9) and states flatly, "No, my daughters. It is more bitter for me than for you, because *the LORD's hand has turned against me!*" (1:13, emphasis mine). Second, when she and Ruth arrive back in Bethlehem "the whole town was stirred because of them; and the women exclaimed, 'Can this be Naomi?'" (1:19). Her response speaks from a heart raw with disappointment and grief.

> She said to them,
>> "Call me no longer Naomi,
>> call me Mara,
>> for the Almighty has dealt bitterly with me.
> I went away full,
>> but the LORD has brought me back empty;
> Why call me Naomi
>> when the LORD has dealt harshly with me,
>> and the Almighty has brought calamity upon me?"
>> (Ruth 1:20–21)

After she has buried a husband and two sons, Naomi is not "okay" with the LORD. And while all the town women want to speak of "pleasantness," Naomi can't go there—not yet. She and the LORD still have work to do.

4. Thorns and Grace: My Story and Yours

I am no biblical figure; I'm not Naomi, Abraham, or Job, but like them (and you) I have a story, one that stands behind and prompts this book. My story, at least this phase, is seven years old and growing. And despite the danger of repeating what you have already read in my first book, the crux of this book requires running the risk of repetition.

My story is about physical pain that has in itself become a disease. After taking a long time to heal from a pesky stress fracture of the third metatarsal bone in my left foot in 2006, the pain stayed on and invited more and more friends to join the party. Based on initial tests the nature of my problem appeared to be the pinching or impingement of a primary nerve feeding into my ankle and foot (the tibial nerve). We waited with hope that the problem would resolve itself. So in spring of 2007 I kept my schedule: I taught my classes, led a retreat for a church, spoke at the Pepperdine University Bible Lectures, presented material at the annual Sermon Seminar hosted by the Austin Graduate School of Theology, and taught for two weeks at the Institute of Theology and Christian Ministry in St. Petersburg, Russia. On the flight home, however, I knew that my body was not healing itself. So I met with my doctor, made the necessary arrangements, and then had (my first) surgery to free-up the tibial nerve, a tarsal-tunnel release in July 2007. I would have my fifth surgery in the fall of 2009 in a last gasp to reduce the pain in my left foot.

In the interim between surgeries it became clear that the initial, innocent stress fracture had set off a neurological firestorm known by different names: Reflex Sympathetic Nerve Dystrophy (RSD) or Chronic Regional Pain Syndrome (CRPS). In RSD or CRPS a minor injury (such as a stress fracture), usually in an extremity (such as a foot), causes the nerves in the surrounding area to become confused so that they continue to send pain signals—even though the original injury has healed. Over time these signals may intensify and even restrict the blood flow to the area as if there is a mortal threat (surgery #3 for me: to cut some of the nerve in order to restore better circulation). The experts disagree about whether or not in some cases the same syndrome with its pain may also spread to the other hand or foot. For me there is nothing to argue about; what began in my left foot and lower leg in 2006 began in my right foot and lower leg in the summer of 2010. Today both feet and calves are completely involved in whatever is happening. So the key for me is pain management—controlling the pain as much as possible without putting my lights out so that I am unable to do anything. There is no cure for these syndromes or possible genetic problems.

I live with pain as a daily houseguest, and I suppose I will for the duration of my life. Some days are not so bad, but most are challenging. I wrote my last work, *Hurting with God*, as a way of lamenting and grieving my pain and the losses it has brought along in its suitcase: an inability to drive more than just a few miles, loss of my administrative position at the school where I teach, and the loss of any hope for future positions (to which I once aspired). There was a time when I preached and taught in churches and seminars across the country; today I can only accept a few well-planned trips. I love the outdoors, and especially bass fishing, but both are difficult propositions today. *Hurting with God* was my own last prayer for God to stop what was happening and restore my life.

Today I feel more like Paul than Job. In 2 Corinthians 12, Paul told the church that he suffered from some unidentified "thorn in the flesh" and that he had prayed three times (three = completely and fully) for God to remove the thorn. In response to Paul's lament God said no: "My grace is sufficient for you, for power is made perfect in weakness" (2 Cor 12:9). To be honest, I don't know what Paul means by "grace" and "power" made perfect in weakness. Frankly, I'd rather have a day or two without pain than get grace that is somehow supposed to be sufficient. At least Job got his health back. Like Paul I've prayed my three days and I know that others have joined me in my prayer. But after seven years, I think it is safe to conclude that God has said no.

It is clear to me that God has said no because of the pain that I still experience in my legs: the deep ache in my calves, sharp electrical pain in my toes, and clamps that compress my large toes. The internal pressure that builds up when I stand makes me certain my feet are about to explode. But worst of all is the pain in most every step I take, and the weariness this pain causes at the end of the day. I may be slow, but I believe it is clear that God has said no to my prayers. Further lament about my pain is useless, a waste of time—and might even tick off God (cf. Deut 3:26).

This is not the place to study how God answers lament or the answers God might give. Sometimes it is painfully easy to know that God has said no—when one's spouse dies, or a child, or a best friend. Then it is time to grieve or mourn (not lament; I will discuss the distinction later). But other times it's not so easy to know how long to keep praying/lamenting for the same thing. We know God told Moses (Deut 3:26), Paul (2 Cor 12:9), and even Job (Job 38:2–3, 40:1–2) to stop pestering him. It is time to move on. So all I know to say is what I argued for in *Hurting with God*: there is a time for lament—fully, completely, wrestling with God and giving God every reason to do what you ask. And this time of lament may last weeks, months, or even years.

When to stop lamenting and move on is a question I have come to expect at every seminar I conduct on *Hurting with God*. And despite ample time to think about the issue, I have no answer that works for everyone. For some, your situation may be like mine and only after years does it become clear that God is not going to bring about healing; or it may take the discernment of groups of wise women and men in your life to know what you should do. My only advice is not to give up too quickly or become impatient with others in their time of lament. If in doubt, have patience and wait, if for no other reason than that the fierce optimism of our culture pushes us to get over times of lament too quickly and get on with life.

We are frightfully uncomfortable spending any more time than we must in "the valley of the shadow of death" (Ps 23:4, KJV); so our goal is to find the bridge that passes safely above the shadows below, or if we must, race through the valley with windows up, doors locked, and a refusal to stop *on that side of town* for anything. And our experience over the past fifty years (or much more) suggests that maybe it is possible to bypass pain. What was major surgery followed by an extended hospital stay twenty-five years ago is now day surgery: in by 8 am out by 5 pm, and back to work in three days. We no longer have to wait anxiously by the phone for news, or worse, wait days in limbo for a letter to announce the fate of a friend or family member. We have computers with email and cell phones with text-messaging; and while yesterday the speed of these devices was staggeringly slow (at the time it seemed incredibly fast), now we become impatient if it takes more than a few seconds to send or receive a message.

Our blessings, however, have turned us into an impatient people, doubly uncomfortable with the time we spend in "the darkest valley" (Ps 23:4, TNIV). If sprinters can run one hundred meters in less than ten seconds, and swimmers continue to break one world record after another, why can't people learn to get past times of lament faster? Sure, people need to lament; but it seems as if they should be able to do what they need to do over the weekend and be back to productive work on Monday, Tuesday noon at the latest.

And for those with faith in God and membership in a community of believers, the pressure can be even greater to pick oneself up, brush off the negativity associated with loss, hardship, or pain, take up greater faith in God's "ultimate plan," and move forward into God's "preferred future." And along with well-intentioned holy encouragement along these lines, our fellow believers are apt to let loose a string of biblical citations indiscriminately set free from their contexts, now flying about the room like a dozen golden snitches smashing against our heads. We need to summon Harry Potter to magically appear, capture the snitches, and put them back where they belong.

Rejoice in the LORD always; again I will say, Rejoice. (Philip 4:4)

> No testing has overtaken you that is not common to everyone. God is faithful, and he will not let you be tested beyond your strength, but with the testing he will also provide the way out so that you may be able to endure it. (1 Cor 10:13)

> My brothers and sisters, whenever you face trials of any kind, consider it nothing but joy, because you know that the testing of your faith produces endurance; . . . (James 1:2–3)

Taken as a whole not only do these texts appear to question Christian lament, they seem to suggest that getting past "the darkest valley" is a simple matter of flipping a faith switch. No matter how traumatic the event that led to lament, it is nothing uncommon or more than you can handle (1 Cor 10:13). Rather, after momentary lament our pain should solicit "pure joy" because God is working in our lives (Jas 1:2–3) toward our ultimate good (Rom 8:28); so we should rejoice—not continue a self-centered lament that questions God's work in our lives (Philip 4:4). After all, what doesn't kill us only makes us stronger (not in the Bible, but it should be).

I discussed the problem with these and other ideas in *Hurting with God* where I made the case for restoring the language of lament in our churches and in our personal faith walks. What I did not talk about, however, was what happens when the time for lament is over; when lament has run its course and, regardless of the outcome, it is time to move on. I did not write about these topics in *Hurting with God* for two simple reasons. First, I ran out of space (thank God). And second, I had no idea what to say.

My work in these volumes is deeply personal, perhaps too much so—but this is my story. *Hurting with God* came out of my own pain and search for God: physical pain that had me to a point of desperation—even if it meant self-amputation. I've been down that road in my mind more than once or twice. But what I needed most of all were words I could use to speak to God, to somehow maintain relationship with God though I was scared, discouraged, angry, and deeply hurt—by God. *Hurting with God* came out of that stage of my journey.

Today I am in a different place. My physical pain is still with me; it's not any better, though on a really good day the meditation, physical therapy, medication, and God's grace grant me short reprieves. Nonetheless, my journey has brought me to a place beyond lament; just how I have gotten here I will discuss later. But for the most part I know that continued lament is not good for me or my relationship with God. It's time to move on. Yet at the same time, I can't move on as if nothing has happened. If nothing else, trying to navigate the world in a custom-built wheelchair is a fairly good reminder that life is not what it was. For a time lament was critical to surviving my journey with faith intact; and *Hurting with God* came out of what I was learning during that time. Today, I am trying to move ahead with my journey—still with the Psalms—learning how to live with God after the time for lament is over. And lesson #1 for the day: sister, this isn't easy.

It is my observation that many people assume: 1) Once God has heard our lament and answered our prayer, the crisis is over and we may resume our lives from the point at which the crisis hit. 2) With the crisis over, we may sing a song or two of thanksgiving with new vigor or add new verses to the old praise songs, but on the whole we return to the faith and faith languages we prayed before the storm hit. 3) As soon as the crisis is past we try to get on with the business of living our lives as if nothing happened. 4) And perhaps most important, we believe that this rush back to our former lives before lament is the most faithful response to the end of lament. It would be highly unlikely that a person or a church would articulate these assumptions. But many do live out these embedded scripts as the crisis they have faced comes to a conclusion.

It is my contention that each of these four assumptions is fatally flawed. Once violent storms push us into seasons of lament they do not go away without inflicting lasting damage or at least changing our relationship with the Divine. Even if God's answer to our prayer was yes, we can no more return to life as it was as Job could return to the days before the LORD made his wager with the Satan, or as Abraham could turn back the sundial before the LORD devised his test, or as Naomi could return to her life before she buried her husband and two sons—or as if I can go back before the very first symptom appeared, or you can go back to when (you can fill in the blank). For better or worse, we are not the same person after our time of lament. Scars remain. And further, how do we *speak* with authenticity to the God who could stop the storm in my life, but chooses not to do so? If we are people of faith and the crisis was serious, then the end of crisis is not the end of the story. It cannot be.

Just as the Book of Psalms provided the words we needed for lament, the Psalter also provides the guidance and language we need for negotiating the time after lament. In what follows we will revisit the language of lament (chapter 2) for the sake of those who have not read *Hurting with God* and as a reminder for those who have in order to set the stage for what follows. Chapter 3 will also consider the lament psalms, focusing primarily on the directions the laments send us as we leave these psalms to move ahead. In other words, the laments set the agenda for what we do after lament—what we say and how we live. Chapters 4–8 examine the directions lament points: trust (chapter 4), thanksgiving (chapter 5), new praise (chapter 6), rejoicing in the Lord (chapter 7), and instruction (chapter 8). Chapter 9 will consider special circumstances within lament and the language after lament, what we may call broken hope for now. Our conclusion, chapter 10, will hold onto our findings in the Psalms as it pushes ahead with practical observations for how we live after lament.

The storms we face in life leave scars: some that will heal in time with proper care, and some that will never go away. Some experiences might make us stronger, and others leave inescapable daily reminders of the past and present struggle to trust God. *After Lament* we do not automatically revert back to the praise songs we loved to sing before our world was turned upside down. The end of lament—be it a dramatic rescue or a deep personal loss, the birth of a long hoped for child or another miscarriage, a complete remission or a peaceful death—the end of lament is not the end of the story. Wherever our lament may lead, it leaves us with stories of pain and scars, reminders of our wrestling with God; and it leaves us in hope—with much to work out with our God.

CHAPTER TWO

What Is Lament?

To talk about the psalms and languages of faith that come after lament without first discussing lament would be like teaching mathematics teachers how to teach without any knowledge of math, or signing a student up for an advanced Hebrew language course when the student doesn't even know the Hebrew alphabet. For reasons we will unearth in this and the next chapter, it will become evident that an understanding of the key features of lament must precede any discussion of psalms that follow an experience of pain and loss; and that without this grounding in lament, these buoyant songs are apt to result in beautiful music that flies away on the wings of shallow theology. Together, lament and psalms that come after lament create a theological whole—two languages so inter-related that one without the other quickly leaves the safety of deep water and heads toward the rocks.

This chapter discusses lament as it relates to psalms that come after lament. Most of this information is in my first book on the Psalms: *Hurting with God* (ACU Press, 2012). Ideally, you will have already worked your way through this earlier book before you move ahead here; but even if you have not, what follows should get you up to speed well enough. And if you have read *Hurting with God*, I still encourage you to stay awake as you read these pages. I've not changed my position, but some ideas are sharpened and some are new. I will begin by documenting the demise of lament, identifying some of the causes for this near-death experience, and considering what this demise means for faith languages that come afterward. Then I will highlight key features of lament, especially those most important for psalms that come *After Lament*. And finally I will consider two examples of lament, one from the Book of Psalms and the other a contemporary enactment of the language.

Part I
The Demise of Lament

The single largest type of psalm in the Book of Psalms is the lament. By my count, the Psalter includes sixty chapters of lament, forty-one hymns of praise, twenty-seven songs of thanksgiving and confidence, and twenty-two other types (see *Hurting with God*, 241–246). For those accustomed to regarding the Book of Psalms as a book of praises, this information can be somewhat unsettling. Why would Israel's book of prayer and song include so much lament (40 percent) as compared to the up-beat songs of praise (28 percent)? Especially when our own hymnals reverse what we find in the Psalter? On average our hymnals (using representative hymnals from Baptist, Presbyterian, and Churches of Christ) are made up by 30 percent praise songs, 38 percent thanksgiving and confidence songs, 15 percent laments, and 17 percent others [though a truer comparison of laments—what we lament for versus what the Psalms lament for—concludes that lament constitutes on average 4 percent of our contemporary hymnals (see *Hurting with God*, 31–41)]. Consequently, what composed 40 percent of the Psalter is now only 4 percent of our hymnals.

The shift from lament (4 percent) to praise and thanksgiving psalms (together 68 percent of our hymnals) statistically supports what we experience week after week in our churches: one praise song after another praise song, interrupted by a prayer of praise as a transition to a special praise song. Lament is a near-dead language, being suffocated to death at the hands of praise songs and up-beat assemblies. Meanwhile those in deep pain, beaten up by the world and lying on the side of the road, are dying for just a word or two of comfort and someone who will speak and argue with God on their behalf. But in our rush to worship in an attractional model, in which our upbeat praise will draw large numbers, we pass by those in pain on the other side of the road (cf. Lk 10:25–37).

Causes for the Demise

1. Misunderstandings of Lament

One cause for the demise of lament is a common misunderstanding of the genre that leads us to think we are lamenting when we are not. This misunderstanding happens in two typical ways. First, on numerous occasions when I have visited a church to speak about lament, worship leaders have told me about the lament service or songs they have planned to go along with my message. These leaders are as genuine in their work as Mother Teresa was in her work; but the worship leaders do not understand lament. They mistake lament to be any song or music that is of a quieter, softer tone than their usual explosive praise songs. Consequently, the worship service is filled with songs such as "Be Still and Know" (Ps 46:1, anonymous), and "The LORD Is My Shepherd" (Psalm 23, The Scottish Psalter, 1650). I love all of these songs for their calm, quiet, and strong affirmation of faith; but they are not laments.

Second, many confuse lament with songs such as one might hear at a funeral, songs of mourning or bereavement: "Amazing Grace" (John Newton, 1773), "It Is well with My Soul" (Horatio Spafford, 1873), or "There Is a Place of Quiet Rest" (Cleland Boyd McAfee, 1903). Once again, I love all of these songs, but they are not laments. It is possible for a song of mourning to also be a lament (e.g., see Ps 90 and the contemporary example below), but most often these are two distinctly different types. A song of mourning grieves what has happened and cannot be changed (e.g., a death), so it lacks requests or appeals for God to do something to change the situation—*now* (a key feature of lament).

2. Calvinism and the Evangelical Will of God

Our usual route to church on Sunday morning passes by one of Abilene's historic trademark buildings—or at least it used to be; a couple of years ago an enormous fire left it nothing more than heaps of charred bricks and a partially intact center elevator or stairwell. Within a week workers erected a new chain link fence to adorn the rubble, with due warning posted against the adventurous who would like to lift a few obsolete bricks engraved with the name Abilene. Workers began to collect salvageable brick onto pallets to be whisked away to a more secure location. And soon thereafter we noticed another addition to the site: a banner attached to what was left of the stair/elevator well that proclaimed, "And we know that in all things God works for the good of those who love him, who have been called according to his purpose" (Rom 8:28).

In Calvinism and much Evangelical theology, everything that happens to us is regarded as the predetermined will of God. So our response to whatever comes should be humble trust and praise of the God who is in control of all things. With just a little attention we can hear people speaking all around us from such a theological commitment. I recently heard about a speaker at the funeral of a young woman; she was under twenty-five with life all before her until another driver ran a stop sign. This speaker tried to convince the crowd that her death was the will of God, that she had fulfilled her life's purpose, and so God took her home. Thank God the two prayers that followed did not fall for such rubbish, but called God to account through lament.

Those who lament believe that life is a free gift of a God who loves and is responsive to prayer. But this God is not a micromanager who provides only an illusion of free choice; we genuinely have free choice—as do others who may affect our lives through their decisions and actions. I understand that we desperately want our world to be under control, especially when life is so completely out of control. But the answer is not that God planned it all and by faith we should accept things as they are. Instead, the laments teach us to bring what's unjust and oppressive to the LORD, and demand with Abraham, "Shall not the Judge of all the earth do what is just?" (Gen 18:25b).

3. Western Optimism

A third overwhelming factor in the demise of lament is the white-knuckled optimism of our churches that refuses to acknowledge, much less deal with, negativity and death (of all types). Churches have avoided contact with the negative psalms—except to use the laments as examples of people who lack faith or who were trapped by sin before the messiah came. For all practical purposes the church has banished these texts that testify to the dark side of human existence. Walter Brueggemann has written extensively about this problem; and his words, though broadly cited in the literature, merit further consideration here.

> It is my judgment that this action of the church [singing praise despite the disorientation of the world] is less an evangelical defiance guided by faith, and much more a frightened, numb denial and deception that does not want to acknowledge or experience the disorientation of life. The reason for such relentless affirmation of orientation seems to come, not from faith, but from the wishful optimism of our culture. . . . I think that serious religious use of the lament psalms has been minimal because we have believed that faith does not mean to acknowledge and embrace negativity. We have thought that acknowledgment of negativity was somehow an act of unfaith. . . . (*The Message of the Psalms*, 51–52)

The disease that has swept across America and the Western world has infected us. A disease whose symptoms include a gospel of health and wealth (as long as we are faithful we will be blessed, but we will suffer if we do wrong—here the Book of Job has been cut cleanly out of the

Bible), and a belief that everything that happens in my life is part of God's detailed plan for my life (see above). So Brueggemann continues:

> The point to be urged here is this: The use of these "psalms of darkness" may be judged by the world to be *acts of unfaith and failure*, but for the trusting community, their use is *an act of bold faith*, albeit a transformed faith. It is an act of bold faith because it insists that the world must be experienced as it really is and not in some pretended way. On the other hand, it is bold because it insists that all such experiences of disorder are a proper subject for discourse with God. (*The Message of the Psalms*, 52)

So then, because of these attitudes and beliefs—both conscious and unconscious—we have minimized lament. In general, we do not use lament psalms in worship. More often, however, worship leaders "mine" the psalms for positive statements, cutting and pasting from the laments until they have created a medley of praise—and a new Book of Psalms more to our own liking. All the while our misunderstanding of lament causes us to believe we are practicing lament when we are not.

4. Catharsis

A final misunderstanding of lament regards the genre to be nothing more than getting everything off one's chest, a cathartic dumping of disappointment, frustration, and rage into the cosmic void. Or, in similar fashion, lament is regarded as little more than complaining, moaning, and groaning about the hardships of life. These are the people that everyone avoids at the company or even church Christmas party. And if you happen to get caught, you learn who your true friend is by who comes to your rescue, pulling you away for some other conversation or task. Pause for just a moment and I suspect you can think of those from the First Church of Moaning and Groaning.

What I have described here is not lament but what Paul might describe as "evil talk" (Eph 4:29) or "abusive language" (Col 3:8). Just complaining about all the terrible things that have happened to you or muttering about how unfair life has become is not, *absolutely not lament.* Just how lament differs from this sort of language will become clear as we take note of the key features of lament, especially the first one.

Part II
Key Features of Lament

1. Conversation

Lament is first and foremost language addressed to God. In Psalm 38, one of my personal favorite laments, it is difficult to read the psalm and not come away with a feeling that we have been eaves-dropping on a private conversation between the psalmist and God. Notice all the words of direct address in Psalm 38: O Lord (1), O Lord (9), O Lord (15a), O Lord my God (1 Lord 5b), O Lord (21a), O my God (21b), O Lord of my salvation (22b). The same personal quality is true for other laments, even the painful and terribly dark Psalm 88: O Lord God of my salvation (1), O Lord (9), O Lord (13), O Lord (14).

2. Needs and Requests

A second key feature of lament is the expression of my needs and how I want God to deal with my struggles. Here I will express the troubles and hardships that I face, often with strong emotion. The difference between this expression and the moaning and groaning we mentioned above is that here we are in a respectful, controlled conversation with God. So, back in Psalm 38, as the poet addresses God, he or she also describes what they are experiencing physically (3,5–8,17), emotionally (10), socially (11–12,19–20), and spiritually: suffering from the Lord's punishment (1–2), awaiting the Lord who will answer (15–16), and confessing, "I am sorry for my sin" (18). But all of these descriptions of physical, emotional, and spiritual pain lead to an appeal, pleading with the Lord not to be so far away (21), but to hurry "to help me" (22). The complaints and descriptions of hardship are present in order to motivate the Lord to come—and hurry to my help.

3. Extreme Cases

Most psalmists admit their own flaws, accuse others of making their situation worse, and indict God for God's failures—because if I praise God for bringing blessings, then ultimately God must be held accountable when, instead of blessing, we are hurt. Such claims against God are present in most laments to some degree. In six of these psalms, however, the writers express raw emotion as they accuse God of gross neglect and wrong-doing (Pss 46, 60, 80, 88, 89, 90). Their charges may be grouped into six indictments:

1. You (God) are inexcusably angry (38:1,3; 60:1,3; 80:4; 88:7,16–17; 89:38,46; 90:7,9,11).

2. You have failed to go out with our armies (44:9, 60:1,10; 89:40,43). Instead you have turned back our sword (89:43), broken down our walls (80:12; 89:40), and empowered our enemies to victory (44:10; 89:42). Because of you, your people are regarded as sheep for slaughter—and massacred all day long (44:11, 22).

3. You have made us suffer hard things (60:3; cf 88:15–16). You have broken us (60:1), crushed us (44:19), shot us with arrows (38:2), and brought your hand down hard on us (38:2–3; 39:10). You made us drink wine that caused us to stagger like a drunkard (60:3), fed us the bread of tears (20:3; cf. 80:5), and gave us tears to drink (80:5–6). You have overwhelmed us with your waves (88:7, 16–17) and your terrors (88:16). You have imprisoned us (88:8), thrown us into the lowest pit (88:6), and plunged us into darkness (44:19; 88:6).

4. You have humiliated us (44:9). You have made us the butt of every joke (44:13–14; 80:6; 89:41) and covered us with shame (89:45). You have caused friends to abandon us (88:8, 18).

5. You have made human life short (39:5), turning us back to dust (90:3), and sweeping us away (90:5). Human life is no more than a vapor (39:5), a dream (90:5), or grass that withers under a hot sun (90:5–6). Because we pass all our life under your anger, our days are only toil and trouble, and come to an end like a sigh (90:9–10); you consume everything humans hold dear (39:11).

6. You have broken covenant (89:39, 49). You have emasculated our king (89:45) and thrown the crown of your anointed one to the ground (89:39, 44). You have rejected your own people (44:9, 24; 60:1, 10; 88:14; 89:38, 46; 90:11)—sold us out for nothing, no profit or cost (44:12), and you have scattered us among the nations (44:11).

It is difficult to believe that poets wrote and said these words to God; and even harder to believe that these words were deemed important enough to merit inclusion in the Bible—both of which should teach us that sometimes such words are appropriate for dialogue with God. God's behavior, according to these psalmists, has been and continues to be indefensible. So they do not hesitate to call God out, without trying to provide some quick explanation that acquits God of wrongdoing or gets God off the hook. Sometimes the problem lies with the actions of others, and the psalmists are equally un-politically correct in their requests of God (see Ps 58). And sometimes the problem is of my own making, and my greatest need is for words of confession (see Psalm 51). Whatever the case may be, the laments provide strong, straightforward language for communicating honestly with God.

4. The End of Lament

Once lament addresses God, describes the problem, and asks for the LORD's intervention (soon), even motivating the LORD by whatever language is at hand, in its conclusion the lament will often move beyond the present crisis with:

1. An expression of trust in the LORD (e.g., 4:8, 12:7, 17:15, 31:24, 40:17, 108:13)

> O Israel, hope in the LORD!
>> For with the LORD there is steadfast love,
>> and with him is great power to redeem.
> It is he who will redeem Israel
>> from all its iniquities. (130:7–8)

2. A pledge to give thanks should God intervene as requested (e.g., 142:7)

> Return sevenfold into the bosom of our neighbors
>> the taunts with which they taunted you, O LORD!
> Then we your people, the flock of your pasture,
>> will give thanks to you forever;
>> from generation to generation we will recount your
>> praise. (79:12–13)

3. A declaration of thanks now, even though there is no indication in the psalm that anything has changed; the poet and his or her community are still under distress (e.g., 7:17, 52:9, 140:12–13).

> With my mouth I will give great thanks to the LORD;
>> I will praise him in the midst of the throng.
> For he stands at the right hand of the needy,
>> to save them from those who would condemn them
>> to death. (109:30–31)

4. A declaration of praise that expresses my confidence in the LORD, even though nothing yet has changed (5:11–12, 13:5–6, 57:11, 59:16–17, 61:8)

> My lips will shout for joy
>> when I sing praises to you;

> my soul also, which you have rescued.
> All day long my tongue will talk of you righteous help,
> for those who tried to do me harm
>   have been put to shame, and disgraced. (71:23–24)

These are not the only movements at the end of or within lament; they are only representative of the range of emotions that may be present. These movements also illustrate the variety of directions in which lament leads its reader to a place other than lament. And here we begin to touch the heart of this book, a theme we will flesh-out in chapter 3 and return to over and over again throughout the book.

Lament is not the end, but the means to an end. We need lament and dare not skip over it as if it were an optional stage on the journey; it is not. But nor should we settle into lament as if it were the final stage of the journey; it is not. Lament helps its reader express what must be said to God; and then, within the same text, lament orients the reader for the next stage, providing steps on a journey that will come *After Lament*. To these ideas we will return in our next chapter; for now we need to turn to examples of lament.

Part III
Examples of Lament

Ultimately, the best way to understand the laments is to read complete examples, with a few brief observations. Above, I mentioned that Psalm 38 is a personal favorite, though that is a relatively recent development. Psalm 38 did not become *my* psalm until I was assigned the translation and commentary of Psalm 36–41 for the *Timeless* project, a three-volume effort to present new translations, short commentaries, and new hymns for the entire Book of Psalms. (The first volume is available. *Timeless: Ancient Psalms for the Church Today, Volume One: In the Day of Distress, Psalms 1–41*, R. Mark Shipp, editor [Abilene, TX: ACU Press, 2011].) As I began work on my assignment, I had already been struggling with chronic pain for three years. By this point almost every step hurt, progressively getting worse through each day. I was just beginning to realize that, like Paul's thorn in the flesh (2 Cor 12:7–10), my pain was not going away. And becoming more biblical by the day, I was also like Jacob, who after his wrestling match at the Jabbok walked with a perpetual limp (Gen 32:31).

As I began to work it became clear to me that whoever wrote the psalm understood pain, and more likely than not, was in significant pain as he wrote this prayer-song. I will spare you all the clues I see that support my claim, except for one: the remarkable description of pain. Ten years ago I would have said all of this language must be metaphorical, that no one could be in such bad physical condition. Today I'm not so sure. As you read the text you will hear the poet say that he feels as if he has been "pierced" by God's arrows and slapped around or hit hard by the LORD's hand (2). He speaks of wounds that "fester and stink" (5) and he walks "bent, stooped so low" by pain (6). Consequently, it as if he is walking in darkness all day long (6b). He feels burning pain (7a) and the sense that his body lacks health (8) or is "completely crushed" (9). Yet, in his burning pain he also feels numb (8a). He has the sense of heart palpitations, a total loss of physical strength, and even failing eyesight (10).

The final image to denote his physical pain resonated with me the most. As I worked with the Hebrew, I checked various translations of verse 17, and then wrote:

> Oh, I go on limping and limping,
> my pain always the next step before me.

I admit translator's liberty, but not much. As I wrote the words to verse 17, I realized I had just translated my own story, what life had become for me: every step an experience in pain. I recognize that many interpreters are quick to dismiss most if not all of the physical descriptions in Psalm 38 as metaphoric—that no one could be that bad off. Humbly, I beg to differ: sometimes it really is that bad. The following text is my own translation:

Psalm 38

A Song for David, for the memorial offering

[1]Oh LORD,
 rebuke me, but not in your anger;
 correct me, but not in your wrath.

[2]Oh, your arrows have pierced me;
 your hand has come down hard on me.
[3]My flesh has no health because of your indignation;
 my bones have no wholeness because of my sin.

[4]Oh, my iniquities have piled up over my head,
 a burden too heavy for me.
[5]My wounds fester and stink
 because of my follies.
[6]I am bent, stooped so low;
 all day long—darkness—I walk.

[7]Oh, my loins are filled with burning pain;
 my flesh has no health.
 [8]I am numb, completely crushed;
 I cry from the groaning within my heart

[9] Oh Master,
 all my desire known to you;
 my sighing is not hidden from you.

 [10]My heart stutters;
 my strength abandons me;
 my sight even fails me.

[11]My friends and my companions
 stand away from my affliction;
those close to me stand far away.

¹²Those seeking my life lay their traps,
    those wanting to hurt me discuss destruction;
    they plan deception all day long.

¹³But I am like the deaf—who cannot hear,
    like the mute—who cannot speak.
¹⁴Indeed, I am like a person who cannot hear;
    and who has no response in my mouth.

¹⁵Oh, it is for you, oh LORD, I wait;
    it is you who will answer, oh Master my God.

¹⁶Oh, I said, "Only do not let them rejoice over me
or when my feet stumble they will boast against me."

¹⁷Oh, I go on limping and limping,
    my pain always the next step before me.

¹⁸Oh, I confess my iniquity,
    I am troubled by my sin.

¹⁹I have so many foes without cause;
    so many who hate me for no reason.
²⁰They repay evil for good;
    they are my adversaries though I pursue what is good.

²¹Oh LORD, do not abandon me!
    Oh my God, do not be so far from me!
²²Hurry to my aid,
    oh Master, my Savior.

Observations

- In addition to the direct address to the LORD (1, 9, 15, 21, 22), Psalm 38 acknowledges that the poet suffers because of his own sin (3–4, 18), the actions of others (11–12, 19–20), and God's anger (1–3).

- Real or metaphorical, the poet suffers from enormous physical illness (3, 5–8, 10, [13–14], 17), social loss (11), enemies out to get him (12, [13–14], 16, 19–20), and spiritual needs (1–3, 9, 15, 18, 21–22).

- His requests, in view of all his troubles, are brief: that God not correct him when God is so angry (1), that the poet's enemies not rejoice over him (16), that God forgive him (18), that the LORD not abandon him or be so far away (21), and that God hurry to his help (22).

- The dire situation the poet describes serves to motivate God into action, as does the situation with the enemy: if God does not respond quickly, the enemies will rejoice (16).

- The poet, despite all his troubles—including his trouble with God—expresses confidence in the LORD: "Oh, it is for you, oh LORD, I wait; it is you who will answer, oh Master my God" (15). To wait is to trust that the LORD will come through with the help so desperately needed.

- So, despite the harsh words spoken to God (1–2), they are words spoken in faith (15) and hope that the LORD will soon come to help (21–22).

This, then, is how those in ancient Israel created their lament psalms. They addressed God with their pain, complaints, and deep needs; oftentimes they suggested ways for solving the complaints and tried to motivate God into action. Then, by the action of a prophet or simply their own faith the poets exclaimed their confidence in God (thanksgiving or praise worked equally as well). Specific references to the situation that would link the lament to a particular set of events are most often avoided; the poets choose not to reveal their historical moment—making their laments ahistorical so that others may use their words. This explanation or recipe for lament seems overly simplistic as I write it; but in fact, lament is not just for the experts who can master a complicated set of skills. The language of lament is for all who approach God by faith in their worst moments and darkest days.

A Contemporary Example: For Liam

The second example of lament is a prayer I wrote by request in January 2012 for Liam's memorial service, a remarkable eight-year-old boy who died from leukemia (T-cell ALL). Diagnosed just over a year before his death, Liam endured chemotherapy, radiation treatments, two stem cell transplants, and an NK-cell treatment. And after the brief hope of remission, every effort to save his life failed.

In July 2011, after another heart-crushing relapse, the family decided to make each day as meaningful as possible by doing three things each day: learn something, make something, and love someone. One day in the conversation Liam learned that nearly a billion people do not have access to clean drinking water—which leads to disease and death. So from a hospital room at St. Jude's Children's Hospital, Liam and his family came upon The Water Project's website and decided to love people they will never meet. Liam decided to do what he could to raise money; and with the help of family and his young friends, within just a few weeks over two hundred people had contributed $16,000—the cost of one well. By October 2011 a second well was completed; and as of this writing Liam's website is still active and had raised over $40,000: thewaterproject.org/liam

During the last month of his life Liam drew many pictures, featured after his passing at the Center for Contemporary Arts in Abilene, Texas, September 1–29, 2012. The drawing on page 48 is one of many pieces featured at the show that, of course, raised even more money for Liam's wells.

Prior to his memorial service the family asked if I would lead prayer, with one directive: speak the truth—what has happened is not okay. I was honored to pray, and give these words to the family. Writing a lament for a child and a family I did not know well took me hours—and took me into the darkness of my own pain; for me there is no other way to write lament. By permission of the family I share those words here.

For Liam

[1]LORD, you have always been our dwelling place;
before the mountains were formed
or the first stars danced with light,
from everlasting to everlasting,
you have been our God.

[2]But LORD, it wasn't supposed to end like this,
gathering to sing a few songs, tell stories,
and share memories of a little boy,
his smile, his art, and his love
for his mom and dad and sister.

[3]So I hope you do not expect us to act
as if nothing has happened,
as if we are not disappointed with you.
[4]How can we help but say,
"If only you had been here Liam
would not have died?"
[5]How are we to get over the death of a child?
At least you got to see your son grow up.
[6]No, everything is not okay. Not with us—or you,
not now, maybe not ever.

[7]Forgive those who think everything is fine,
who are eager to assert your good reign.
[8]Strike dumb those who would dare to say
this was your will, a part of your plan.
[9]Restrain those who would rush to affirm
that all things work together for good.
[10]If you, God, can do all things, then couldn't you
accomplish your good without this grief?

[11]O LORD, we are broken;
we grope about in darkness.
[12]We cannot deny our pain,
and yet we find that we cannot deny you.
[13]This we call to mind,
   and therefore we have hope:
[14]The steadfast love of the LORD never ceases,
   your mercies never come to an end;
[15]they are new every morning;
   great is your faithfulness.

[16]We have seen your mercies in the most unexpected places.
   [17]We've seen a little boy more concerned
about his parents than for himself.
[18]We've seen that because of Liam
families in faraway places have a better chance
   of seeing their children live.
[19]We've seen parents live with amazing hope
   and relentless courage.
[20]We have seen glimpses of your faithfulness.
   [21]But what we most wanted, we did not receive;
glimpses of mercy have not been enough.

[22]LORD, we prayed so much for Liam, for this family;
   now we hardly know what to say;
nor anywhere else to go but to you.

[23]You have much work to do here,
and we call you to it.

[24]LORD, grant Matt and Amy your peace for today,
your strength for tomorrow,
and courage for years to come.
   Catch them in your arms when they fall.
[25]Grant Gary and Sandy, Roddy and Nancy grace

> to love and shepherd their children.
> Hold them as they watch and remember.
> [26]Grant your church the loving discipline
> to walk alongside this family—
> confused by your mysterious absence,
> refusing to let go of your love.

For the sake of the following observations I have numbered the verses in Liam's prayer.

Observations

- As typical of lament, the psalm/prayer directly addresses the LORD throughout the prayer (1, 2, 10, 11, 22, 24).
- The prayer tries to motivate God to action by describing the remarkable ways Liam and his family coped with his illness (19–20), including his love for people on the other side of the world (16–18).
- As also occurs in the Psalms, Liam's psalm alludes to or cites other portions of scripture.
  - Verse 1 cites Psalm 90:1–2.
  - Verse 4 alludes to the resurrection of Lazarus (John 11:28–44) and quotes John 11:32.
  - Verses 7–10 alludes to the misuse of Romans 8:28.
  - Verses 13–15 are from Lamentations 3:21–23.
- The prayer is honest in its expression of disappointment with God (2, 3–6, 21).
- Despite the harsh words directed to God (2–6, 10, 21–23), the prayer also expresses confidence in the LORD (1, 12–15) as it makes its requests, both general (7–10) and personal (23–26).

More than a few jaws dropped when I read this lament at Liam's memorial service; but most important, the family affirmed that these were the words they needed to say to God on that awful day. Later, I have been told, those who were initially shocked realized that the lament expressed what they were thinking and feeling, but did not know how to express.

Untitled 1—Liam Lowe, January 4, 2012

Conclusions

To learn and use the language of lament may mean reading a lament psalm from the Bible at an appropriate moment, or it may mean learning how to write your own lament. More than anything, lament is being honest with God, which is one mark of a good relationship. What is just ahead in chapter 3 is a careful study of how the laments conclude and where the laments lead their readers. For example, in Liam's prayer the key verses at the beginning (1), middle (13–15), and end (24–26) lead or encourage the reader to trust in the LORD, despite all that has happened that might cause a person to turn and walk away from the LORD.

My journey is now ready to leave lament in search of new direction(s), new language(s), and new way(s) to live with God in my circumstances of pain. Naturally, I invite you to come along in your own journey and walk with God, to find a new language and direction that comes after lament. My spiritual discernment recognizes that it is time for me to move on—beyond lament. To what? I do not yet know. But I know I must reexamine the psalms of lament and discern where they lead a person like me, where I am to go, and what I am to say after my lament.

So before moving ahead, if you are reading this during a time of lament in your life, I challenge you to consider carefully whether or not it is time to look ahead just yet, or time to remain as you are. In other words, given our culture's unease with darkness and times of lament, do not let our culture push you to get over lament when you are not ready. Wait. Be patient. You can read the rest of this book later. Allow yourself time to work out whatever you need to work out with God. If you need the help of wise counsel, seek it out. And then, when you know you are ready, come ahead with me to chapter 3: "The Wheel of Lament."

CHAPTER THREE

The Wheel of Lament

L ament is a language in motion. But where lament is leading the reader is an open question. Most writers on the topic, including my earlier work, conclude that lament leads primarily to thanksgiving (*Hurting with God*, 177–178). And to be sure, some lament psalms declare that they will give thanks for God's help (e.g., Ps 52, 57), render thank offerings (e.g. Ps 26, 56), or urge their readers to give thanks (e.g., Ps 44, 79, 140). We can even identify some thanksgiving songs that were written as a response to an earlier promise in lament to give thanks (e.g., Ps 30, 116). Nonetheless, the primary direction in which the psalms of lament take their writers and their readers is not thanksgiving. In this chapter we will trace the different directions lament takes their readers, and discover the language and position to which most laments lead. But for at least a moment, we need to sit with the news and reflect on the reality that thanksgiving is not the destination at which most of us will arrive.

This news can scarcely be surprising; it squares with what experience has taught us to be true: not every prayer is answered as we had hoped, especially the most important prayers spoken in the middle of the night in hospital rooms and emergency wards. I doubt we need hard data to support what we intrinsically know. And yet, in my experience (and yours), what we know to be true about our prayers and life has yet to make a dent in our practice when we come together in worship. The songs we sing would give any outsider the impression that our prayers must find thanksgiving to be our normal response to God's actions.

One way to imagine the different directions in which the lament psalms lead their readers (and writers) is to picture lament as an old wagon wheel with a center hub from which radiates several spokes. The center hub is where the common theme of trust unites all of the laments. Each spoke is woven into the hub with trust while adding its own ideas that point out from the hub in different directions to the rim which holds the psalms that come after lament. In other words, for the laments, trust in the LORD is incontestable. But the crisis that precipitated the lament may yet turn out in several different ways, each of which will require a different response in addition to trust. The wagon wheel reminds us that the ultimate goal of lament is to move beyond itself.

Two Necessary Technical Matters

1. Before continuing on to the directions in which the poets of lament psalms lead their readers, two technical matters demand our attention. First, it is to be expected that the spokes pointing outward, away from lament, share overlapping ideas. Directives to give thanks are found alongside the motif of teaching (86:11–12), just as the content of the third spoke (praise) is found with encouragement to give thanks (the second spoke; e.g., 9:1–2, 35:18, 69:29–30). Consequently, the decision of where to include some laments is subjective, based on the perceived strength of the ideas in the psalm. In other words, whichever idea

seemed stronger to me determined the placement of the psalm. Let the arguments begin!

2. The second technical issue with direct impact on our study is the notorious difficulty of translating the tense of verbs in the Psalter. Due to the nature of the Hebrew verbal system, in some psalms a single verb might be translated as complete, present, or future action. Consequently, how the verb is translated is a subjective educated decision on the part of the translator or team of translators. For the sake of consistency in this study I use the New Revised Standard Version for all translations of the psalms. Though I might quibble with some of their decisions regarding the verbs, on the whole I find their decisions to be among the best.

Spoke #1: Trust and Confidence

Of the sixty chapters of lament in the Psalms, only nineteen mention thanksgiving or a thank-offering as the goal or eventual outcome of their prayer.[1] On the other hand, fifty-one of these same sixty chapters set their readers on a course to trust, wait, hope, take refuge, or, as expressed in various metaphors and figures of speech, to rely on the LORD.[2]

The center axis common to the laments is trust or reliance on a God who is dependable and trustworthy. This confidence is present throughout other spokes of the wheel, but exists in what might be called a "pure form" in the first spoke. These psalms express confidence in the LORD alone, without mentioning other actions such as we find elsewhere (e.g., to praise or give thanks). To be sure, relying on God when everything is at stake is an action, though of a different nature than

---

[1] Laments that mention thanksgiving or a thank-offering as the hopeful outcome: Ps 7:11, 9:1, 26:7, 28:7, 44:8, 52:9, 54:6, 56:12, 57:9, 69:30, 79:13, 86:12, 108:3, 109:30, 140:13, 142:17.

[2] *To trust:* 4:5, 9:10, 13:5, 22:4, 25:2, 28:7, 31:6,14, 52:8, 55:23, 56:3–4,11, 62:8, 77:5, 86:2, 143:8; *to wait:* 4:4, 25:21, 31:24, 38:15, 62:1,5, 130:5; *to hope:* 39:7, 62:5, 71:5, 14; *to take refuge:* 5:11; 7:1, 17:7, 25:20, 57:1, 61:3, 64:10, 71:1,3,7, 62:8, 141:8, 142:5, 144:2. See other images for hope in Ps 2, 3, 31, 44, 59, 60, 62, 63, 69, 70, 74, 77, 89, 108, 109, 140.

singing new praise, rejoicing in the Lord, or receiving instruction from the LORD. In fact, trusting God to come through when the odds are stacked against me is far more difficult to do than singing a song of thanksgiving because God has already saved me.

Fourteen psalms belong to this first spoke of pure trust. Five of these psalms include only one or two verses of spoken confidence in the LORD (6:9–10, 17:6, 15, 38:15, 39:7, and 60:12). On the one hand, despite their brevity the writers of Psalm 6 and 17 appear to be quite confident in the LORD and his imminent help. On the other hand, the brief statements of confidence in Psalms 38, 39, and 60 reflect a greater struggle: when, if ever, will God help? (We will return to these three psalms in Spoke 6.) The majority of the psalms in this first spoke, however, include substantial statements of faith in God's reliability (2:4–9,11e, 3:3–8, 12:5–7, 55:16–19, 62:1–2,5–7,11, 74:12–17, 77:11–20, 85:8–13, 130:3–4,7–8).

What assures the writers (and readers) of the LORD's provision in these psalms is consistent with what we will see and develop further in other spokes.

1. If You Say So. In Psalm 12 an oracle of salvation (12:5) is the basis of trust in God (12:6–7; see also 4:4–5).

2. Remember. In Psalm 77 everything changes when the writer determines to remember: "I will call to mind the deeds of the LORD; I will remember your wonders of old. I will meditate on all your work, and muse on your mighty deeds" (77:11–12). Consequently, memory of God's past faithfulness enables the psalmist and reader to place trust in the LORD despite strong present evidence against the LORD (77:1–10; see also Ps 85 and 74).

3. The Lord Reigns. Psalm 2 and 55 recognize the LORD as the true king (2:1–9, 55:19), and this awareness prompts their exclamations of trust.

> Cast your burden on the LORD,
>   and he will sustain you;

He will never permit
>the righteous to be moved. (55:22)

4. Now and Forever. It might be as simple as in Psalm 3, 62, and 130; the existing faith of the psalmists orients them toward an assured reliance on God in the present and future.

>Trust in him at all times, O people;
>>pour out your heart before him;
>>God is a refuge for us. (62:8)

Regardless of how, we find on this spoke an amazing trust in the face of knee-shaking, heart-pounding danger. Their trust is not the result of a lesser threat, but the consequence of a saint's faith. We mortals salute them.

Spoke #2: Thanksgiving Psalms

Since we have already mentioned thanksgiving, we turn to this next spoke on the wheel (Pss 7, 26, 28, 44, 56, 57, 79, 108, 109, 140, 142):

>I will give thanks to you, O LORD, among the peoples;
>>I will sing praises to you among the nations. (52:7)

>With a freewill offering I will sacrifice to you;
>>I will give thanks to your name, O LORD, for it is
>>good. (54:6)

Thanksgiving is a fundamental attitude and action in relationship with the Divine, as well as any other healthy relationship. Find a marriage that has gone a few years without either spouse speaking words of gratitude, look closely and then ask yourself if that's what you would want. So, in their own way, the lament psalms that constitute this spoke work to develop a culture of gratitude wrapped around the core value of trust. The question is how these psalms with their complaints and requests lead readers to thanksgiving? To answer this question three factors stand out.

A. What's Begun Is as Good as Done

The lament may lead its reader to thanksgiving by identifying a small event that foreshadows the Lord's complete salvation. Thus, while still aching for complete deliverance, the psalmists interpret the event as the beginning of what the Lord will do and summon the reader to give thanks now for what God has started and will most certainly finish. For example, in Psalm 57 the writer opens with an appeal for God's mercy while, at the same time, confessing trust in the Lord: until the storms pass by, the poet will take refuge in the shadow of God's wing (57:1). From this protected place she continues to cry out for God Most High to save, while danger still lurks like a lion (1–4). Then God's deliverance begins to take tangible form: the enemies are caught in the trap they set for the writer (6; on the identity of the enemies see the discussion in chapter 5). With this good news the psalmist senses that complete deliverance is just around the corner, so she sings with confidence:

> My heart is steadfast, O God,
> > my heart is steadfast.
> I will sing and make melody.
> > Awake, my soul!
> Awake, O harp and lyre!
> > I will awake the dawn.
> I will give thanks to you, O Lord, among the peoples;
> > I will sing praises to you among the nations.
> For your steadfast love is as high as the heavens;
> > your faithfulness extends to the clouds.
> > (Psalm 57:7–10)

With the end of the crisis in sight the psalmist leads the reader in this warm-up exercise for the full-bodied thanksgiving to come when God finishes his work. In similar fashion, Psalm 7 regards the enemies falling into their own trap (7:15–16) as an indicator that God's victory ("righteousness") has begun. Consequently, like Psalm 57, he writes, "I will give to the Lord the thanks due to his righteousness, and sing praise to the name of the LORD, the Most High" (17). Of course it is possible that the psalmists may misinterpret what they see, that God's deliverance has not yet begun; nonetheless these writers dare to interpret their world through the eyes of faith—God is on the move (see also Psalm 44:6–8, 56:12–13, and 54:6–7).

B. Let's Make a Deal

The second concept that prompts or enables the laments to lead their readers toward thanksgiving is a conditional clause in which *if* the LORD will deliver, *then* they will express thanks. For example, in Psalm 79 the writer describes the defilement or destruction of the Jerusalem temple (79:1–4) before asking God to reverse his policy, to pour out his anger on the nations (5–7) and have compassion on his own people (8–12; with harsh wishes against the enemy). The psalm continues, "*Then* we your people, the flock of your pasture, will give thanks to you forever; from generation to generation we will recount your praise" (79:13; emphasis mine). Here, thanksgiving depends wholly on God's response to the prayer, a response that, unlike group A above, has not yet begun. It is only if and when God comes through for the psalmist and reader that thanksgiving will begin.

Three other laments use the same rhetoric. In Psalm 142 the writer asks the LORD to "Bring me out of prison, *so that I may give thanks* to your name" (142:7, emphasis mine). Psalm 140 presents a wish list of actions for God to take against the writer's enemies (140:6–7) and confesses strong trust in the LORD: "I know that the LORD maintains the cause of the needy, and executes justice for the poor" (12). Then the poet concludes, "Surely the righteous shall give thanks to your name; the upright shall live in your presence" (13). Nothing has begun to happen; but if or when it does, then the righteous will be ready to give thanks. Finally, Psalm 109 also follows the same hopeful, but conditional pattern. Despite the problematic nature of the psalm (the identity of the speaker in vv. 6–19 is unclear; is it the poet or the enemies?), it is only after God saves the writer and shames the enemies as the psalmist asked (109:26–29) that he will give thanks (30).

Such psalms are vulnerable to the charge of foxhole religion or bargaining with God to get what you want. And truth be told, both charges are on target and to be acknowledged without shame or discomfort. These writers trust their God and write from a strong relational position. Consequently they are not above using whatever means possible to motivate God to act on their behalf. If God wants their thanksgiving, their gratitude, then God is going to have to do what is praiseworthy.

C. If You Say So

Finally, the mood changes in this spoke when someone steps forward to speak on behalf of the LORD. In Psalm 28 the writer begs for God to hear (28:1–2) and fears being labeled with the wicked (3). He asks that God repay the wicked according to their work (4). Then, unexpectedly in verse 6, the poet exclaims that the LORD has heard his appeal and declares that the LORD is "my strength and my shield . . . with my song I give thanks to him" (7). The explanation for how the writer moves from desperate appeals in verses 1–4 to overwhelming confidence in verses 6–7 turns on the words in verse 5:

> Because they do not regard the works of the LORD,
>   or the work of his hands,
> he will break them down and build them up no more.
>   (28:5)

While it is possible that the psalmist wrote these lines in confidence that the LORD had heard his appeal and was going to act as requested, it seems much more likely that this verse belongs to another voice. On behalf of God a priest or prophet has stepped forward with the LORD's message—which changes everything for the psalmist (and reader).

The second lament that pushes its reader toward thanksgiving in the same way is Psalm 108 (an edited combination of Psalm 57:7–11 and

60:5–12). Here the writer begins with thanksgiving (108:1–6), until the LORD's speech is recalled:

> God has promised in his sanctuary:
>> "With exultation I will divide up Shechem,
>> and portion out the Vale of Succoth.
> Gilead is mine; Manasseh is mine;
>> Ephraim is my helmet;
>> Judah is my scepter.
> Moab is my washbasin;
>> on Edom I hurl my shoe;
>> over Philistia I shout in triumph." (108:7–9)

Unlike Psalm 28, however, this oracle leads not to confidence but to questions:

> Have you not rejected us, O God?
>> You do not go out, O God, with our armies. (108:11)

Then, after a request for help in battle (because "human help is worthless," 12b), the psalm concludes with confidence, just as it began:

> With God we shall do valiantly;
>> it is he who will tread down our foes. (108:13)

On this first spoke, then, psalmists lead their readers to thanksgiving by identifying small places in which God's kingdom or rescue has already begun to break through in triumph, setting forth conditional clauses that bind thanksgiving to God's intervention, and recording words from God that create confidence that breaks out in thanksgiving. These may be initial words from a physician that our child is going to be okay—and we collapse in tears of gratitude. Or it might be recognizing other ways and places in which the kingdom of God is breaking through in new ways.

Spoke #3: Sing a New Hallelujah

The motif of praise in the laments is not only strong on the basis of how often praise or a related idea occurs, but how strong the idea becomes in some of the psalms themselves. For example, in **Psalm 71**, a lament for old age or growing older and those who are trying to take advantage of those who are no longer strong (71:9–13,17–21), this writer declares his praise of God over and over throughout the psalm.

> My praise is continually of you. (6e)

> My mouth is filled with your praise,
> and with your glory all day long. (8)

> But I will hope continually,
> and will praise you yet more and more. (14)

> I will come praising the mighty deeds of the LORD God,
> I will praise your righteousness, yours alone. (16)

> I will also praise you with the harp
> for your faithfulness, O my God;
> I will sing praises to you with the lyre;
> O Holy One of Israel.
> My lips will shout for joy
> when I sing praises to you
> my soul also, which you have rescued. (22–24)

While this elder servant of the LORD makes a strong appeal for God's help, and he desperately needs God's help (9–13), it is equally clear that his praise is not tied to the outcome of the event. Saved or not, this saint will praise the LORD; and what's more, by using his words he encourages all who read, pray, or sing his psalm to do the same: praise the LORD regardless of the present situation. Therefore, Psalm 71 belongs to the first sub-group of laments that lead their reader to praise.

A. No Matter What

In the same way as Psalm 71, Psalm 59 and 69 are also determined to render praise (59:16–17; 69:31,34–35) despite difficult circumstances (59:1–15, 69:1–29) even though God has not yet begun to correct what is wrong. The most exceptional example of this group, however, is Psalm 89. The text begins with praise:

> I will sing of your steadfast love, O LORD, *forever*;
>> with my mouth I will proclaim your faithfulness *to all generations*.
> I declare that your steadfast love is established forever;
>> your faithfulness is as firm as the heavens. (89:1–2, emphasis mine)

This psalm continues for another thirty-five verses calling the heavens to praise the LORD's faithfulness (5) while God's people "exult in your name all day long, and extol your righteousness" (16). But all is not what it appears to be. The praise is either a set-up or mighty act of faith in view of what comes next. The promises God made have been broken; not just cracked, but smashed like a watermelon falling off the back of a speeding truck. The heir of all those good promises, the Davidic king, has been caught in the eye of a storm. God has renounced the covenant (39), taken away his support in battle (42–43), and opened the city for anyone who would like to plunder it (40–41). It is a good day to be an enemy of Judah/Israel (42). And lacking a United Nations to file an appeal, the psalmist protests to the only court available: the same LORD who has withdrawn his support (46–48). All he can do is ask the LORD what happened to his love and faithfulness (49–50). The psalmist's world has collapsed and his God has gone AWOL. And yet, this same writer begins the psalm, "I will sing of your steadfast love, O LORD, *forever*" (1a, emphasis mine). Psalm 22 presents the same dramatic shift in reverse; it moves from intense complaint (22:1–21a) to unbridled praise (22b-31).

Finally, at least two psalms urge or guide their readers to sing praises in the present—now, and in the future (Ps 9–10, another psalm divided into two chapters, and Ps 61, discussion omitted here). In Psalm 9–10 the psalmist begins with a strong unconditional affirmation that she will give thanks, tell of all God's wonderful deeds (9:1), and be glad and exult in God: "I will sing praise to your name, O Most High" (9:2). The poet also urges others to sing praises "to the Lord who dwells in Zion" (9:11). Then, however, the psalmist 1) asks the Lord to see her suffering on account of "those who hate me" (9:12a), and 2) affirms that God is "the one who lifts me up from the gates of death" (9:12b), "so that I may recount all your praises, and in the gates of daughter Zion, rejoice in your deliverance" (9:14). Psalm 61 is a lament with strong trust that God will hear and do what the psalmist asks. The psalm concludes with a promise for today and every day, "So *I will always sing praises* to your name, as I pay my vows day after day" (61:8, emphasis mine).

B. Remove the Barrier

Other laments that lead their readers to praise consider praise to be a future outcome only if God will hear and respond to their requests. It is not, however, that these writers do not want to praise the Lord; something is preventing their ability to praise. Psalm 42–43 (a single psalm divided into two chapters) holds out the hope that in the near future the poet, perhaps a musical director (42:4, 43:4), will no longer be cut off from the temple (?) but will again be in a position to "praise him, my help and my God" (42:5b–6a, 42:11b, 43:5). Then, but only "Then I will go to the altar of God, to God my exceeding joy, and I will praise you with the harp, O God, my God" (43:4; cf Ps 63 and 144). Psalm 102 also regards praise as a desirable outcome, but in this case, praise awaits the future restoration of Jerusalem. After the lament's complaint—which may represent an individual, the king, or the city (102:1–11)—the poet affirms that the Lord is enthroned as king (12) and that the Lord will restore Zion because its appointed time has come (13); God will build up Zion and appear in his glory (15) which will lead to praise and worship (21–22). But in this case the poet fears that he will not live long enough to see these spectacular events; he is mortally ill because God has lifted him up and thrown him aside (3–10). Standing between the writer and praise in the temple is God's restoration of the poet's health and restoration of the temple.

Spoke #4: Rejoice in the Lord

The concept of joy or rejoicing has been present in three psalms considered above (Pss 5, 51, 90) in which other themes predominate. A small group of psalms, however, exclusively or primarily urge the reader to rejoice and/or exult in the LORD or the LORD's salvation.

A. Let's Make a Deal (II)

In **Psalm 64** the writer describes the problems created by the wicked (64:1–6); then the writer or perhaps some other person (e.g., a prophet?) confidently proclaims that God will shoot down the enemy and bring him to ruin (7–8). As a result, "*then* everyone will fear" and talk about what God has done (9, emphasis mine). Then, the psalm concludes, "Let the righteous rejoice in the LORD and take refuge in him. Let all the upright in heart glory." In a similar fashion, **Psalm 58** promises God that *if* he will act swiftly to establish justice (in a fierce manner, vv. 1–9), "the righteous will rejoice *when* they see vengeance done" and will even participate in the victory by bathing their feet in the blood of the wicked (10, emphasis mine).

B. No Matter What

Psalms 31 and 70 each establish a simple relationship between the command to rejoice and their present crisis. Early in **Psalm 31** the writer says, "I will exult and rejoice in your steadfast love, *because* you have seen my affliction; you have taken heed of my adversities and have not delivered me into the hand of the enemy" (31:7-8a, emphasis mine). But then a substantial lament follows (9–24) which details personal distress and sorrow (9–10), social loss (11–13), and continued appeal to the LORD for help (14–18). The writer expresses resilient faith through it all: he testifies to how the LORD takes care of those who take refuge in him (19–20), he remembers the time when the LORD exceeded all of his expectations and came to help (21–22), and finally, he encourages those who are hurting:

> Love the LORD, all you his saints.
>> The LORD preserves the faithful,
>>> but abundantly repays the one who acts haughtily.
>> Be strong, and let your heart take courage,
>>> all you who wait for the LORD. (31:22–23)

No matter what may happen, this writer will trust in the LORD (6), making the LORD his rock, fortress, and refuge (1–4), committing his spirit into God's hands (5), and rejoicing in the LORD's steadfast love (6). More simply, **Psalm 70** describes and requests help from God against enemies who seek the life of the psalmist (70:1–3). Then at the end of the psalm the writer urges all who seek the LORD to "rejoice and be glad in you. Let those who love your salvation say evermore, 'God is great!'" (4), despite the fact that at this point the LORD has not yet delivered anyone yet (5). No matter what may happen, Psalm 31 and 70 urge their readers to "Rejoice in the Lord always; again I will say, Rejoice" (Philip 4:4).

Spoke #5: Instruction

The fifth spoke or direction in which the laments lead their readers is to appeal for God to teach or lead them. For example, as a common lament **Psalm 25** addresses the LORD (25:1), describes a difficult but vague threat (11, 19), and makes several requests (2–3, 6–7, 11, 16–22) among which forgiveness stands out (7,11,18). Within this framework the writer begs the LORD to instruct and lead her.

> Make me to know your ways, O LORD;
>> teach me your paths.
> Lead me in your truth, and teach me,

> for you are the God of my salvation;
> > for you I wait all day long.
>
> Good and upright is the LORD;
> > therefore he instructs sinners in the way.
> He leads the humble in what is right,
> > and teaches the humble his way.
>
> Who are they that fear the LORD?
> > He will teach them the way that they should choose.
> > (25:4–5,8–9,12)

Also within the context of forgiveness (86:5, 90:8, 143:1–2), Psalms 86, 90, and 143 ask the LORD to instruct and lead them.

> Teach me your way, O LORD,
> > that I may walk in your truth;
> > give me an undivided heart to revere your name.
> > (86:11)
>
> So teach us to count our days
> > that we may gain a wise heart. (90:12)
>
> Teach me the way I should go,
> > for to you I lift up my soul.
>
> Teach me to do your will,
> > for you are my God.
> Let your good spirit lead me
> > on a level path. (143:8b,10)

Two other psalms with the motif of instruction differ from this model of sin-forgiveness-request for instruction. In Psalm 5 the poet requests the LORD to lead her because dangerous and wicked enemies surround and threaten her (5:8–10). And in Psalm 51, back within a clear context of sin, confession, and forgiveness (51:1–12), the writer reverses the idea and proclaims that if God will forgive, *the psalmist will teach* other sinners God's ways so they will return to the LORD (13).

Spoke #6: Broken Hope

I mentioned above that three psalms in Spoke #1 expressed minimal confidence in the LORD due to what appears to be a faith struggle within the psalmists (38:15, 39:7, 60:12). In **Psalm 38** the writer describes *physical collapse* ("no soundness in my flesh" [38:3], wounds that "grow foul and fester" [5], "utterly spent and crushed" [8], strength fails [10], and unending pain [17]), *social loss* (friends and companions have abandoned him [11]), *ruthless enemies* (people seek his life by laying snares and plotting his ruin [12] to which he has no chance to respond or save himself [13–14]; these people are eager to rejoice over his downfall [16], which appears to be imminent [17]—though they have no cause for their hatred, they are returning hatred for the psalmist's love [19–20]). The poet also describes *God's anger*, which is out of control and killing the poet (1–2); the writer is sorry for and confesses his sin (4–5,18), but in his anger God seems not to notice. Consequently, even though he appeals for God's help (16, 21–22), his confidence that God will save is low. Only one verse expresses genuine hope: "But it is for you, O LORD, that I wait; it is for you, O LORD my God, who will answer" (15). These words are remarkable, especially in view of a God who is fuming, using the psalmist for target practice, and slapping the psalmist around with an abuse of divine power (1).

Psalm 39 is even less hopeful. After a time of not speaking in prayer for fear of the words that might come out and what God might do (39:1–3), finally the words escape (39:4–6): human life is no longer than a few inches (5) and God is beating the psalmist senseless (10). He knows God's response is due to human sin (11), but even so—to make life so short and then assault and take away everything humans love (11)—what kind of God is this? The poet's final requests cut with precision: 1) hear and "do not hold your peace at my tears" (12); 2) I am a passing guest, an alien in your presence—an unspoken appeal to God's own laws for treating an alien with kindness (see Lev 18:33–34); and 3) if God refuses to live by his own rules, the poet asks God to leave him alone for just a little while: "Turn your gaze away from me, that I may smile again, before I depart and am no more" (13). In the middle of these harsh charges against God, a lone verse holds out hope: "And now, O Lord, what do I wait for? My hope is in you" (7). Like Psalm 39, hope is present, but it is held by a thread (see also 60:12).

Eventually, threads snap and the sixth spoke breaks off from the hub. The spoke may remain connected to the outer rim (the community?), or may be in the ash-heap beside Job. But this spoke is broken and lacks the core-value that enables lament to roll forward: hope. Faith remains, but the vibrancy of hope for a life beyond lament is gone. The writers and readers still turn to God, appeal to God, and cling desperately to God because they have nowhere else to go. But explicit statements of trust are gone, and with these the buoyant hope we find in other laments is lost to the current. For these saints, happy-go-lucky songs about "How Great Is Our God" with the praise band rocking into one more encore of the chorus are—to borrow terminology from the Old and New Testament—99.9 percent dung. We have prayed three times with Paul, and our thorns are not going away (2 Cor 12:7–9). Just what do you want us to say in your praise and worship service?

Several psalms that we have already studied and/or assigned to another spoke might be nominated as candidates for admission into this sixth spoke: harsh laments that explicitly hold God accountable for the collapse of their world and lives (Ps 44, 60, 80, 88, 89, 90), or docile laments that express few if any explicit words of trust or hope (e.g., 120, 123, 141). Acknowledging my subjectivity, I accept the candidacy of two psalms.

The first psalm, **Psalm 88**, comes out of a time comparable to the collapse of the twin towers, Wall Street, and the housing market—all on one day; sorry Job, but you have just been upstaged. Even worse, to the writer, God has turned on his own people with an anger that overwhelms like a flood (88:7, 16–17). He has abandoned his people to the Pit (4–5), stripped away every friend (8, 18), and refused to respond to prayers that come every day (9)—morning (13) and night (1–2). This writer is not ready to give thanks to a God who delivers, because he is desperate to be delivered from the terrors of a God he has always trusted (13). And he does not understand:

> O LORD, why do you cast me off?
>> Why do you hide your face from me?
> Wretched and close to death from my youth up,
>> I suffer your terrors; I am desperate.
> Your wrath has swept over me;
>> your dread assaults destroy me.
> They surround me like a flood all day long;
>> from all sides they close in on me. (88:14–17)

What is utterly amazing here is that the speaker's troubles and the source of these troubles (the LORD) does not silence the speaker or take away his faith. He cries out into the darkness (1, 18) even if the darkness refuses to respond.

The second text, **Psalm 137**, comes well after the collapse, when ideas such as hope were left behind years ago when the LORD stood aside and watched Babylon burn down his house (the temple), destroy the city's protection (the walls), and carry us into exile (2 Kgs 25:8–11). And then, just to add insult, our captors asked us to sing one of the joyful songs celebrating the Zion—as it lay charred and in ruins (137:1–3). How could we (4)? So we hung up our harps and imposed two curses. The first is a self-curse: should I/we forget Jerusalem is our highest joy (6b) let my right hand wither (5, which would be the end of any harp playing) and let my tongue stick to the top of my mouth (6, which will be the end of any singing). We refuse to sing the happy songs of the kingdom and God's good reign when our world and lives lie in a wreck.

The second curse in this psalm comes in the verses that typically get all the attention in Psalm 137:

> Remember, O LORD, against the Edomites
>> the day of Jerusalem's fall,
> how they said, "Tear it down? Tear it down!
>> Down to its foundations!"
> O daughter Babylon, you devastator!
>> Happy shall they be who pay you back
>> what you have done to us!
> Happy shall they be who take your little ones
>> and dash them against the rock! (137:7–9)

Barbaric, inhumane, unimaginable, and also highly unlikely ever to happen. Babylon is far too strong and our God was too weak to stop Babylon in the past, here on our own soil; so how could the LORD help anyone overthrow Babylon anyway? The harsh, grotesque language testifies to a lack of hope.

Conclusion

Our survey has yielded important results for understanding the laments and the psalms that come after lament. Lament is, in fact, a language on the move, not content to sit before God in a constant state of self-pity or file never-ending charges against the Divine. Lament guides, directs, leads, and pushes the reader toward a new language and a new life with God. Which direction and what language, however, largely depends on God. Based on the laments *we may expect thanksgiving to be a possible, but not probable outcome.* Our outlines of the Psalms must be changed on this point. Some believers may move from Disorientation to New Orientation, or from lament to thanksgiving, but only some. A larger number must learn to live in trust or even praise of the God who does not deliver. We do not get to decide the direction we get to go. God is in the lead, and the next step is up to God; so we follow God's decision (if we disagree with God, the floor is still open for debate).

There is nothing more maddening in our world of fast food, fast cars, fast computers, and faster internets than: 1) to be tied to a schedule other than my own, and 2) for that schedule to be slow. After I wrote the book on lament and taught among churches, the one reliable question I could count on from the audience was this: But don't we need to move on? Isn't there a danger in allowing lament such a large place in our liturgy? Some people never stop complaining as it is.

We live in a culture that values what moves fast, whether a car that moves from zero to sixty in 5.0 seconds or the wife who grieves her life-partner over the weekend and come Monday is ready to get back down to business. "What a woman of faith," we say. Putting down the family pet seems to permit more time for grief. Or we just don't understand why some people seem to take forever to move past their divorce, their child's death to leukemia (may it be a thousand times damned), or neuropathy that keeps a person in daily pain and exacts its toll every day in lost energy, lost independence, lost hobbies, even a lost physical ability to sing praise. So let's get this straight: a fast spirituality does not equal a good spirituality. Be patient with yourself; be patient with others in their losses.

The other gain from our survey is identifying the directions in which lament leads. Even with an obvious overlap in themes, the laments write the directions on the compass for us to follow in our study of the Psalms after lament. Consequently, our next six chapters follow the compass left to us by lament: chapter 4—psalms of trust and confidence, chapter 5—thanksgiving psalms, chapter 6—a new hallelujah, chapter 7—rejoicing in the Lord, chapter 8—psalms of instruction, and chapter 9—broken hope. Whether such a journey into the Psalms is possible or productive is yet to be seen, but at least we will follow the tracks where lament leads, even if we find trails grown-over by neglect.

CHAPTER FOUR

Spoke #1: Psalms of Trust and Confidence

Moses had just begun to lead Israel's family out of Egyptian slavery when an emergency develops that nearly ends the trip before they get off the driveway. Pharaoh has changed his mind again, and is coming in full force to track down Moses and the people and put them back to work where they belong. The people see and "in great fear" (Exod 14:10) cry out to the Lord and complain to Moses, "We told you so" (a generous paraphrase of 14:11–12). Moses responds, "Do not be afraid, stand firm. . . . The Lord will fight for you, and you have only to keep still" (14:13–14). Don't panic. Don't run. Trust the Lord to handle the threat.

Fast-forward Several Centuries

Hezekiah, king of South Judah, had a decision to make. He had just seen what Assyria had done to North Israel—in fact, there is no more North Israel. And now the threat was standing outside his city gates. Assyria has sent a letter: surrender or else. But Hezekiah knew that the crisis was really of a different nature. So he took the letter to the temple, unrolled the scroll in the presence of the Lord, and prayed (2

Kgs 19:14–19). When he was done a message came from the prophet Isaiah, including this line: "He shall not come into this city, shoot an arrow there, come before it with a shield, or cast up a siege ramp against it" (2 Kgs 19:32). Hezekiah's task? No different than what Moses told the people hundreds of years before: trust the Lord to handle the problem.

We do not give ancient Israel enough credit for standing in front of the super-powers of her day—and trusting the Lord. And now it is our turn as we see that the key ingredient in the spokes leading out from lament to new languages and ways of being is nothing less than trust in the Lord. Whether, as we will see, the lament leads us to thanksgiving, new praise, rejoicing in the Lord, or instruction—trust facilitates every movement after lament. Trust welds each spoke to the hub of the wheel, supports each spoke, and here forms a spoke of its own: psalms that begin and end with resolute trust in God.

In this spoke a few of the psalms offer one or two verses of confidence (6:9–10, 17:6,15, 38:15, 39:7, 60:12) but most provide substantial affirmations of God's reliability. For example, in Psalm 74 a catastrophic event has occurred, which leads the writer to ask if God has cast his people off forever (74:1)? The sanctuary is in ruins while the foe scoffs and speaks of complete subjection (3–11). Then the psalmist begins to remember:

> Yet God my King is from of old,
> > working salvation in the earth.
> You divided the sea by your might;
> > you broke the heads of the dragons in the waters.
> You crushed the heads of Leviathan;
> > you gave him as food for the creatures of
> > the wilderness.
> You cut openings for springs and torrents;
> > you dried up ever-flowing streams.
> Yours is the day, yours also the night;
> > you established the luminaries and the sun.

> You have fixed all the bounds of the earth;
> > you made summer and winter. (74:12–17)

Essentially, my God can do anything! In a similar case from Psalm 3, the foes are beyond number, and they claim that there is no help coming from the poet's God. But the writer remembers and rests in the LORD's security.

> But you, O LORD, are a shield around me,
> > my glory, and the one who lifts up my head.
> I cry aloud to the LORD,
> > and he answers me from his holy hill. *Selah*
> I lie down and sleep;
> > I wake again, for the LORD sustains me. (3:3–5)

Like many others, the poet realizes that he has no need for fear or to waste sleep in useless worry (see 2:4–9 11;12:5–7; 55:16–19; 62:1–2, 5–7, 11; 77:11–20; 85:8–13; 130:3–4,7–8).

As also demonstrated in chapter three, what assures these writers that they can rely on the LORD is either: 1) an oracle of salvation from the LORD (e.g., 12:5), 2) remembering the LORD's past faithfulness (e.g., 77:11–12), 3) recognizing that the LORD reigns and therefore may be relied on for deliverance (e.g., 55:19,22 and 74:12–17 above), or 4) the psalmist's existing faith leads to an assured reliance on the LORD now and always (e.g., 62:8 and 3:3–5 above).

Twelve Psalms of Trust

On the wagon wheel, the fourteen laments of spoke #1 that urge their readers to trust the LORD also lead us to psalms that come after lament that emphasize reliance on God: 11, 16, 18, 20, 23, 27, 41, 46, 91, 121, 125, and 131. My selection is subjective, made on the basis of content or subject matter, not form-critical analysis. A brief aside for the non-specialist: form-critical identification of psalms is akin to determining where our songs originate and their original usage in that setting. For example, the work of Erhard Gerstenberger (*Psalms 1 and 2*) demonstrates the diversity of genres among my twelve psalms. He categorizes these twelve psalms as:

- Songs of confidence (16, 46, 125, and 131)
- Liturgies and rituals of various types (20, 23, and 27)
- A psalm of contest (11)
- A messianic thanksgiving song (18)
- A complaint of the individual (41)
- A benediction preached to a community in worship (91)
- Words of assurance/pilgrimage song (121)

Of course, not all scholars agree with all of Gerstenberger's decisions (e.g., see the form-critical assignments in the three volumes on Psalms by Peter Craigie, Marvin Tate, and Leslie Allen in the Word Bible Commentary series). With this said, once again I emphasize that my selections are made on the basis of subject matter.

Beginnings

Most of these psalms begin with palpable exclamations of trust, reaching out for their place in the wheel.

> I love you, O Lord, my strength.
> The Lord is my rock, my fortress, and my deliverer,
> > my God, my rock in whom I take refuge,
> > my shield, and the horn of my salvation,
> > my stronghold.
> I call upon the Lord, who is worthy to be praised,
> > so I shall be saved from my enemies. (18:1–3)

> The Lord is my light and my salvation;
> > whom shall I fear?
> The Lord is the stronghold of my life;
> > of whom shall be afraid? (27:1)

> God is our refuge and strength,
>> a very present help in trouble.
> Therefore we will not fear, though the earth should change,
>> though the mountains shake in the heart of the sea;
> though its waters roar and foam,
>> though the mountains tremble with its tumult.
>> *Selah* (46:1–3)

> The LORD is my shepherd, I shall not want. (23:1)

These four exclamations, representative of the twelve psalms, draw evocative word pictures of a an impregnable fortress surrounded by enemies who do not yet realize the futility of their presence (18:1–3 and 46:1–3) and a personal God who safely leads the poet and reader through danger (27:1 and 23:1).

As above, I think the most beneficial or advantageous approach to these psalms is to ask questions of the group, instead of selecting only two or three representatives for close reading. Our questions, naturally, will probe the source and nature of the writers' confidence in God.

Claims to Relationship

The twelve psalms of confidence use twenty personalized metaphors (e.g., "my shepherd") or direct claims (e.g., "my help") to depict God's past and present relationship to the psalmist. Most images presume warfare or the threat of a battle in which the psalmist faces superior forces. Many metaphors envision a secure place from which the psalmist may engage the battle or retire from the fight in safety.

- My refuge (91:2)
- My fortress (91:2, 18:2)
- My rock (*sl*`, 18:2)
- My rock (*tsvr*, 18:2b,46)
- My stronghold (*msgb*, 18:46)
- The stronghold of my life (*m*`*vz*, 27:1)

Still within the field of battle, on two occasions the writer describes God as an object of protection.

- My shield (18:2b)
- My Light (27:1)

Most often, however, the poets refer to God's involvement in the conflict in more direct terms. In these cases God is:

- My strength (18:1)
- My deliverer (18:2)
- My salvation (27:1)
- God of my salvation (18:46, 27:9)
- Horn of my salvation (18:2b)
- My help (27:9)
- My support (18:18b)

Finally, sometimes setting aside a metaphor or extending it, the psalms declare the LORD to be:

- My God, in whom I trust (91:2)
- My God, my rock [see above] in whom I take refuge (18:2)
- by my God I can leap over a wall (18:29b)
- My LORD; I have no good apart from you (16:2)
- The LORD, my God, lights up my darkness (18:28)
- The LORD is my chosen portion and my cup (16:5a)

It is noteworthy that these particular metaphors in these twelve psalms are in a defensive rather than offensive position. With these brief metaphors God's people are not on the attack, but exercising self-defense. The poet of Psalm 46 stretches our imaginations even farther, painting part of the mural with a vision of the end of war.

> Come, behold the works of the LORD;
>> see what desolations he has brought on the earth.
> He makes wars cease to the end of the earth;

> he breaks the bow, and shatters the spear;
>> he burns the shields with fire.
> "Be still, and know that I am God!
>> I am exalted among the nations,
>> I am exalted in the earth."
> The LORD of hosts is with us;
>> the God of Jacob is our refuge. (46:8–11)

The Vision of War No More

The vision of no more war is full of hope, but challenged by other texts within the twelve psalms of confidence. To begin, **Psalm 20** is a blessing for a king and his army as they leave for war. It is possible that their mission is of a defensive nature, but those who offer the blessing are concerned, not for defense, but for victory:

> May we shout for joy over your victory (20:5a)

> Now I now the LORD will help his anointed;
>> he will answer him from his holy heaven
>> with mighty victories by his right hand. (20:6)

> Give victory to the king, O LORD;
>> answer us when we call. (20:9)

Toward the goal of victory, the blessing asks for the LORD's help to be sent directly from the LORD's throne in the sanctuary in Zion (20:3, 4, 5c, 6). And in a shrewd move, the poet slips in a reminder to the king and his troops that the key to their victory is not their strength or possession of the newest in warfare technology (20:7); their strategic advantage to victory is their trust in the LORD.

In **Psalm 18** the king (or less likely, an individual) boasts in the divine training and equipping he has received from the LORD (18:31–35, cf. Eph 6:11–17). He then speaks of pursuing and overtaking the enemy.

> I struck them down, so that they were not able to rise;
>> they fell under my feet.

> For you girded me with strength for the battle;
>> you made my assailants sink under me.
> You made my enemies turn their backs to me,
>> and those who hated me I destroyed.
> They cried for help, but there was no one to save them;
>> they cried to the LORD, but he did not answer them.
> I beat them fine, like dust before the wind;
>> I cast them out like the mire of the streets. (18:38–42)

The writer credits his victory to the LORD and for this victory he promises to "extol you, O LORD, among the nations, and sing praises to your name" (18:49).

Psalms of Trust and Confidence

A Sampling

It's not unlike the dire predictions we hear all around us, that every generation has heard pronounced with solemn dignity: What will become of us now? What can the righteous do if Obama is elected? If McCain and Palin are elected? With the same anxiety, one voice in **Psalm 11** has assessed his situation in Jerusalem or Samaria (or Cleveland) and concluded that the foundations of society are crumbling (11:3); and the righteous are in mortal danger. The wicked are not waiting around, but marking, aiming, and about to fire at the righteous (2). So the verdict is clear: run for your life! Or, stated with more poetic beauty, "Flee like a bird to the mountains" (1b). After all, if the foundations of society are crumbling, "what else can the righteous do?" (3b). *What are we going to do?*

Another voice speaks in Psalm 11, a voice of faith—of one who has taken refuge in the LORD (11:1a), and who cannot understand the frenzy: "how can you say to me, 'Flee like a bird to the mountains' (1b). I don't think this believer is naïve or unable to see the troubles confronting society. This believer is not blind. In fact, this believer is the only one with clear vision that puts matters into true perspective:

The Lord is in his holy temple;
  the Lord's throne is in heaven. (11:4a)

The Lord reigns. Corrected vision enables us to see the Lord on a throne, not off on vacation while the world goes to hell in a back pack loaded with a bomb. God is watching, testing, and discerning who is righteous and wicked (4b-5). And God has his own plans for the wicked (6) and the righteous (7).

Psalm 11 brings us good news: all the energy we are spending running from one place to another like Chicken Little, crying about the sky falling or about the flaws of this generation, or about the righteous foundations of our nation crumbling—we can all give it a rest. God is on the throne—and that is enough.

An American Psalm: Psalm 23

In the epilogue to his book *The Psalms through Three Thousand Years* (Minneapolis: Fortress, 1993), William Holladay writes about "How the Twenty-third Psalm Became an American Secular Icon." And he points out, strangely enough to our ears, that Psalm 23 carried no special popularity in the states before or during the Civil War. Psalm 91 held some esteem, but not Psalm 23. But then, by the time of Spanish-American War (~1898), Holladay writes, "The psalm [23] was a cliché for dying soldiers" (362). Within three decades, between 1865 and 1895, Psalm 23 had become part of American secular culture and was well on its way to fame and fortune. Holladay attributes this movement to two triggers. The first was a tribute to the psalm, only two paragraphs articulated by Henry Ward Beecher (1813–1887), who was the Billy Graham or Max Lucado of his day. The tribute, part of a longer sermon or lecture, speaks of the powerful comfort Psalm 23 has provided. Beecher wrote:

> The twenty-third psalm is the nightingale of the psalms. It is small, of a homely feather, singing shyly out of obscurity; but, O, it has filled the air of the whole world with melodious joy, greater than the heart can conceive. Blessed be the day on which that psalm was born...It has charmed more griefs [sic]

to rest than all the philosophy of the world. It has remanded
to their dungeon more felon thoughts, more black doubts,
more thieving sorrows, than there are sands on the sea shore.
(*Life Thoughts*, 8–10)

Beecher's tribute was printed and reprinted, summarized, spoken, and
read to American audiences who then began to look at this powerful
psalm for themselves.

The second trigger was the inclusion of the psalm in Louisa May
Alcott's enormously popular *Little Women* (1868). Chapter 40, in which
the family, especially Jo, accepts Beth's impending death is entitled "The
Valley of the Shadow"—a clear allusion to Psalm 23:4. And then near
the end with Jo at her bedside, Alcott describes Beth's death "as Father
and Mother guided her tenderly through the Valley of the Shadow, and
gave her up to God."

These two triggers alone are not able to sway culture; other factors
most certainly came into play. Holladay suggests and then provides
analysis of what he describes as three interwoven developments. "The
shift from the old Calvinist theology into both liberal theology and
individualistic evangelicalism; the feminization and sentimentalization
of both church and culture; and the continued evolution of "civil religion" (365). Agree or disagree with Holladay's analysis, Psalm 23 has
become an American Protestant favorite—from birth to the grave. And
I expect that it will continue to be so for long into our future—which
testifies to the literary art of the psalm.

The shepherd (and sheep) of Psalm 23 live in two different worlds.
On the one side we have green pastures, calm water, and good paths to
get from one place to the other, sometimes passing through deep, dark
valleys that frighten me—a sheep. What kills sheep comes out of the
dark or happens when sheep wander away into the woods. But "I fear
no evil" (4) for two reasons: 1) you are with me, and 2) I know from the
last time, and the time before that, and the time before that I don't need
to worry. The Lord is capable and will protect me.

The second world of Psalm 23 is in the city, indoors—not outside; at a table set for two—just you and me. No enemies allowed; they can only watch. You refresh me with oil to anoint my head and a cup that overflows with wine. (Sorry Welch's, but we are still at least two thousand years away from the processes that will enable us to fill my cup with grape juice. And if someone is backstage cutting my wine with 50% water my cup is not going to be all that refreshing.)

In the second world the LORD is still a shepherd, but in the ancient Near Eastern sense of the word—the shepherd as king. And so it is here, in the courts of the king I will live out my life in complete safety.

Unto the Hills: Psalm 121

Coming or going? Fear or faith? Questions surround the opening lines of **Psalm 121**:

> I lift up my eyes to the hills—
> from where will my help come?

As it now stands, Psalm 121 is the second of a group of psalms (120–134) with the superscription or heading: "A Psalm of Ascents." The phrase most likely denotes a group of pilgrimage psalms collected for those traveling to the temple for some special occasion. The poet or traveler looks up toward the hills, the hills on which the city stands or perhaps the hills between him and his destination: the hills that inspire trust (cf. 123:1, see Hossfeld and Zenger, 321–322), or a journey through hills that creates fear (cf. Lk 10:29–37). And he asks, "from where will my help come?": the words of an anxious pilgrim looking toward the hills ahead, or a reminder that these hills (of Zion) are the source of help. The ambiguous question, however, finds a confident answer in verse two: "My help comes from the LORD, who made heaven and earth."

At this point a new voice enters the psalm with a single message: the LORD keeps (*shmr*) you; God's people are a "kept" people. Emphasis by means of repetition follows as the verb occurs six times in six verses (3–8).

- "He who keeps you" will not become drowsy (3)
- "He who keeps Israel" will not slumber or sleep (4)
- "The LORD is your keeper" (5a)
- "The LORD will keep you" from all harm (7a)
- "The LORD will keep your life" (7b)
- "The LORD will keep" your coming and going, now and always (8)

The key term "keep" (*shmr*) takes various nuances of meaning, as demonstrated by this psalm: unlike other gods, Israel's guard and watchman does not grow drowsy or drift off asleep on the job (3–4), the LORD prevents harmful ("evil") things from happening to Israel (7a), the LORD protects your life (7b), and Israel's keeper will look after them now and always (8).

Verses five and six introduce another related metaphor that transports us to other ancient beliefs and fears. The maker of heaven and earth (1), "your keeper," is also "your shade" on your right side (5). On the one hand, God's shade protects from the harsh sun during the day (5a). And on the other hand, God's shade also protects from the moon at night (5b). Moonlight was regarded as potentially as dangerous as sunstroke; it might cause mental disturbances. Our vocabulary attests to our own past fear of the moon with such terms as "moonstruck," or "lunatic" (from the Latin, *luna* = moon). But, the psalmist claims, our keeper is our shade from any such attack, at all times, day or night.

Finally, it is difficult to read Psalm 121 without thinking of the blessing Aaron and his sons were to pronounce on Israel: "The LORD bless you and *keep you*" (Num 6:24, emphasis mine). The following verses define what it means for the LORD to bless and keep Israel: Instead of fear from the sun or moon striking Israel (Ps 121:5–6), "the LORD make his face to shine on you, and be gracious to you; the LORD lift his countenance upon you, and give you peace" (Num 6:25–26). Faith not fear marks the one who follows the LORD, the one whom the LORD keeps.

A Woman's Point of View: Psalm 131

Psalm 131 also belongs to the Psalms of Ascents (Pss 120–134). Short and sweet, each verse constitutes a major thematic movement in the psalm.

1. The opening verse consists of a three-part denial of pride and of the lifestyle that accompanies arrogance and its pretense.

> O Lord, my heart is not lifted up,
>> my eyes are not raised too high;
> I do not occupy myself with things
>> too great and too marvelous for me. (131:1)

The heart and eyes are commonly associated with pride in the Old Testament: "Haughty eyes and a proud heart—the lamp of the wicked—are sin" (Prov 21:4, see also 6:17, 18:12, 30:13). Even today we describe prideful people as *looking down* on others. The third denial also has to do with pride, reaching above one's status in order to appear more important.

2. If, for the moment, we accept the NRSV translation of the ambiguous and contested text in verse two, the author of the psalm may be female.

> But I have calmed and quieted my soul,
>> like a weaned child with its mother;
>> my soul is like the weaned child that is with me.
> (131:2)

Two terms in this translation do not make good sense in the context. First, the phrase "my soul" (NRSV, *nephesh*) would be better translated "my life" to avoid Christian misunderstanding of the term. Second, a two to three year old weaned child (*gml*, NRSV—"weaned") is not especially calm or quiet in his or her mother's lap, or with any one else. Instead, another sense of this key term suggests a child who has *finished nursing* for now, not for all time. A nursed child is at ease on his or her mother's breast; such a picture conveys the calm, serene, and total trust in God the text tries to convey. If these changes to the NRSV are correct, the female authorship of Psalm 131 is without doubt.

> But I have calmed and quieted my life,
>> like a nursed child with its mother;
>> my life is like *the nursed child that is with me.*
> (131:2, author's translation)

While a weaned child of two to three years old is not especially content to be calm or quiet (on which the extended metaphor depends), a nursed child or baby is content. Mothers can recall the feeling of a nursed baby in their arms, completely content, at rest, cooing, or perhaps even sleeping.

3. The final movement of the psalm begins with language from the previous psalm, "O Israel, hope in the LORD" (Ps 130:7a).

> O Israel, hope in the LORD
> from this time on and forevermore. (131:3)

The writer knows for Israel to set her hope in the LORD she must give up her pride and become like a child, walking away from the race to attain a name and learn to trust God. Just as a later rabbi would teach:

> He called a child, whom he put among them, and said, "Truly I tell you, unless you change and become like children, you will never enter the kingdom of heaven. Whoever becomes humble like this child is the greatest in the kingdom of heaven. (Matt 18:2–4)

A Refuge and Strength: Psalm 46

Our final example, **Psalm 46**, opens with a fundamental faith claim; the rest of the psalm then works out the implications of the claim on our lives. The claim is simple:

> God is our refuge and strength,
>> a very present help in trouble. (46:1)

God is . . . words we dare not race past in a hurry to what we deem to be more important or complex theological matters. Here, unpacking this sentence, we have finally reached the center of our quest to find a language and a way to live with God after lament.

God is our refuge (makhaseh). A refuge is a place of protection and security—and in the Psalms, the only genuine place of refuge is God or with God. In addition to Psalm 46, many other psalmists claim refuge in the LORD (e.g., 11:1a, 16:1a, 31:1a, 71:1a), some describe God as a strong rock of refuge (18:1–2), others describe refuge as a place of safety under the shelter or shadow of God's wings (61:4, 36:7b, 57:1,91:1–2,4), or under a reliable battle shield (18:30, 144:1–2). As the psalmists employ the metaphor and think of God as their refuge, their most common request is naturally for protection (7:1,16:1a, 17:7, 25:20, 31:19, 141:8b). And consequently, those who take refuge in the LORD are rescued (37:40), redeemed (34:22), happy, and sing for joy (2:11e, 5:11a, 34:8,64:10a). It is far better to take refuge in the LORD than to trust in mortals, especially the promises of princes (118:8–9).

God is . . . our strength ('oz). Throughout the Psalter the psalmists lead the chorus of praise for the LORD's strength, which in and of itself is worthy of praise (e.g., 21:13, 29:1, 62:11-12a, 93:1, 96:6–7). More important to the psalmists, however, is how the LORD uses his strength. After all, if power corrupts and absolute power corrupts absolutely, then no one is at greater danger of corruption than the LORD (first), or those with access to the LORD's power (second). So the LORD's strength is a matter for prayer or praise as the LORD uses his power to save those in need, whether his anointed king (21:1, 28:8), his people (28:8, 29:11, 68:28,35, 81:1a), or a psalmist in need (59:9,17, 86:6, 118:14a, 140:7). No strength, real or imagined, stands opposed to the LORD. And while the psalmists admit the LORD's power creates fear—"your enemies cringe before you" (66:3)—the LORD's strength also spurs hope for peace (29:11), happiness (84:5), and love (59:17, 62:11-12a). So, it is no surprise that other writers urge their readers to wait for the LORD who will be their strength (31:24), or more actively seek the presence of the LORD and his strength (105:4).

God is . . . a very present help (*'ezrah*). I would prefer to rewrite this final claim. Instead of a "present help in trouble" after the fact, I wish God kept trouble away, keeping it locked up so that it cannot touch us or those we love (and since we are to love everyone, that covers just about everyone on the planet, though I'm still holding out on a couple of people). That's what we want, but not what we get; and I have no good explanation for why life is filled with so much pain. This year a man was sleeping in his bed when a sinkhole opened under his room—and he falls one hundred feet to his death. This summer nineteen firefighters from the Granite Mountain Hotshots lost their lives when the wind suddenly changed directions, trapping them with no escape route. I understand our desire to understand why these things happen. But frankly, I'm suspicious of anyone who claims to have the answers. Even the Bible is not all that clear. Instead of answers, we are offered God's help.

The psalmists spend a good bit of energy on this topic—calling for the LORD to help (12:1, 30:10, 35:2, 44:26, 79:9, 108:12, 109:26,86), begging the LORD to hurry without any further delay (22:19, 38:22, 40:13,17, 70:1,5,12) and providing testimonies to God's help (10:14, 37:40, 54:4, 63:7, 86:17, 118:7,13, 121:2, 124:8, 146:5).

> God is our refuge and strength,
>   a very present help in trouble. (46:1)

Therefore, we do not fear. Regardless of what may change my world or in my world; no matter what may rock my world or stir-up the primeval waters of chaos so that nothing holds. We will not be afraid.

To read Psalm 46 requires equal parts of imagination and faith. By faith and imagination we live in the city of God, a city fed by a sure and steady river—and God is at home in the middle of the city. This city is not going anywhere; God will be around to help in the morning. So let the nations be in an uproar and kingdoms shake over the latest threat.

When God awakes in the morning he will see and speak a few words—and the earth will melt (back into place?).

> The LORD of Hosts is with us;
>> the God of Jacob is our refuge. (46:7)

Venture outside the city to look about the world, where the LORD has been at work with his "desolations" (8). He brings wars to an end. Imagine deeply, freely. He has broken the archers' bows, shattered the gruesome spears, and what we see burning are either shields (NRSV) or war chariots (author's translation). Can we imagine it: peace on earth? So instead of our frenetic running, much of which is driven by deep fear, the psalm challenges us—God himself challenges us:

> Be still, and know that I am God!
>> I am exalted among the nations,
>> I am exalted in the earth. (46:10)

But this is the trouble with trust—and all language and life with God after lament for all but those lucky ("blessed") few to whom God listened and answered their lament. None of us want to have to trust God; we want matters to go our way so that trust is superfluous. So we have a nice song to pull out and sing on Sunday, but not what I have to live on Monday. What I want is a God who will listen, answer, and then accept my thanks for doing what I wanted. Or what I would really like is for God to pay close enough attention that I never need lament. I am glad to sing about trust; I just don't want a life that requires trust.

> The LORD of Hosts is with us;
>> the God of Jacob is our refuge. (46:11)

To live in God's world demands an act of great imagination: to believe that God is our refuge, our strength, and our help—when our prayers go unanswered, falling back to the ground with our tears. To believe God is our refuge when we bury our children. To imagine God is our strength when we have no strength left for the struggle and power is aligned against us. To see God is our help when pain and disease refuse to go away, even when morning dawns (5). To have the faith and imagination in which the LORD is still competent to break machine guns, shatter rockets and smart bombs, and burn all the shields that keep us from trusting in God alone.

Like Psalm 46, to live without fear requires imagination and great trust in what cannot be seen, because what can be seen discourages and frightens. The psalmists knew this to be true of their world and their faith—and this is why their laments stressed trust above all else. Whether the next move was the fulfillment of a vow and song of thanksgiving or, as is more often the case, the next move is the praise of a God they must trust. Praise in these laments does not mean that the poet knows that God will do what has been asked (as we have too often assumed). Praise is the sublime practice of trust. God's people sing praise with joy, not because all has gone their way, but because they are practicing imaginative hope and trust. The church testifies to this faith by being filled with broken people whose only shared experience of God is God's failure to act, and whose only shared experience of faith is imaginative hope that God is still our refuge, our strength, and our help.

CHAPTER FIVE

Spoke #2: Thanksgiving Psalms

I wish that my laments led to thanksgiving, to a New Orientation; I wish the same for your laments. Wouldn't it be wonderful if the only language we needed after we prayed for help was thanksgiving? That God would be like *Bruce Almighty* and set the auto-reply on his prayer computer to "yes"—or that the odds would at least be better than a Las Vegas slot machine. Four times I lay in a pre-operative bed waiting with prayers that this time this surgery would take away the pain. And four times neither the prayer nor the surgery led to thanksgiving. More than three times I have prayed for God to remove this thorn in my flesh and restore all the losses it has brought (cf. 2 Cor 12:7–9). And God has said no; either that or I have a rotten sense of timing—every time I have prayed God has been on the back nine and didn't want to be disturbed. I understand that God has more pressing problems in this world than one person with severe chronic pain; the Middle East, Afghanistan, and a good bit of Africa comes to mind, not to overlook believers in China and North Korea. But it also seems to me that my request would take little divine effort to remedy, just a touch (cf. Matt 9:20–21). What is it God? Can you not spare even a nanosecond or one angel needing to earn Halo credit?

Thanksgiving is the language of the blessed, the fortunate whose prayers in the deep of night find a hearing with the LORD in the divine council, with a delegate immediately dispatched to the scene. These graced folk may not get everything they wanted or just as they wanted, but they know that God has heard their prayer and answered. They know what it feels like to be surprised by joy and discover New Orientation. And they are the ones who should be writing this chapter. To put my cards on the table, it is difficult for me to write about thanksgiving psalms when I am in pain—now. I find the task to be akin to asking me to write a dog-training manual, when my Basset Hound—Buford Hercules—and I have a friendly agreement: he will sit, if it involves food, and play dead, as long as he can find a comfortable place to die and roll over onto his back to get his belly scratched. Otherwise, anything goes; I am powerless to persuade seventy-five pounds of low-set Basset Hound to do anything other than what he pleases, when he pleases.

Please do not misunderstand. I am thankful for many things: Dana, the surprise of my life who said "yes" and seven months later "I do"—and I am still amazed. I am grateful for T'auna and Steven, Taylor and Simeon, David and Lannea, and Wade (and for the grandchildren to come some day). I am grateful for a job that I love and that I can still do, for the most part, despite the pain. And I am grateful for days when the pain stays on a low hum, like the static on a television instead of needles, electrical sockets, or coals of fire. I am thankful for many gifts and recognize that I am spoiled beyond my recognition. Even so, it's just that when it comes to the one thing I most want today, which affects everything else in my life, my God has said, "No."

So, out of my own quest to find a language for and relationship with the Divine after lament, I begin with a language that is not my own, but one that is nevertheless the logical next step for our study. What we hope for in lament is for God to rescue or heal, or answer us however we need so that our response to God turns into bold and shameless dancing in gratitude before the throne (cf., 2 Sam 6:12–15). And perhaps it is this hope that has led us to presume that thanksgiving is the next step after lament, or that New Orientation always comes after Disorientation. Or maybe it is the wishful optimism of our culture that with hard work and great faith every disaster will lead to an even greater success.

I don't want to make something more complicated than necessary, but it does appear that we have some misunderstandings about the thanksgivings psalms and how these texts inform our practice of thanksgiving. So we begin with a "pentateuch" of five preliminary observations to keep in mind as we move ahead.

Preliminary Observations

1. Genesis

Thanksgiving is not a creation *ex nihilo*, out of nothing, with no pre-existent material or background story. Rather, a word or act of thanksgiving presupposes a recent specific crisis and someone who dared to help. Consequently, in the Psalms, the laments that direct us toward thanksgiving are not thinking in terms of our developing an Attitude of Gratitude or some such character adjustment (even if most of us could use it). Nor are they pushing us to change our perspective on life; yes, I know that there are many people who live with pain much greater than my own, but that is not the point. Rather, the writers expect that we are responding to something God has done—here and now. Recall the sub-group of lament from chapter three that lead toward thanksgiving: *What's Begun Is as Good as Done, Let's Make a Deal,* and *If You Say So.* In every case these laments expect God to do something before we applaud with thanksgiving. God must break into our world in response to our lament and act in an undeniable fashion. Call it a miracle or not, my guess is that in most cases it's not as "miraculous" as most people define the term. But when God decides to get involved, thank you comes to our lips as naturally as we stand to watch a homerun fly over the centerfield fence to win the game in the bottom of the ninth inning.

So if your God stopped doing anything visible in this world around the end of the first century, you can sit this one out—your life has little to do with thanksgiving. Or if lament is not a part of your church's common practice you may skip ahead three spaces to the next chapter (where the same problem will appear) or return to Go, collect $200, and start again with lament. Thanksgiving *presupposes lament*; and *without lament, thanksgiving makes little sense*. As defined by the Psalms rather than our frenetic worship, thanksgiving is an act in reaction to what God has done because of and in response to our lament/prayer.

2. Exodus

Chapter three and four dethroned thanksgiving as the only, primary, or even first direction set by lament psalms. Against common assumptions, we found trust, not thanksgiving, to be the primary aspiration and direction of the laments. Thanksgiving supposes that we got what we wanted, the object of our lament. In fact, however, there are, at most, ten thanksgiving psalms in the Psalter ([18] 30, 41, 92, 107, 116, 118, 124, [136], 138) and about the same number of laments that lead or encourage the reader to give thanks (7, 26, 28, 44, 56, 57, 79, 108, 109, 140, 142). To be sure, the composers wrote these psalms to be used by many people in many different situations. Nonetheless, based on the limited number of laments leading to thanksgiving and the short supply of thanksgiving psalms, it appears that the writers and/or editors did not expect that many people who asked for God's help were going to get what they asked for—and thus need a thanksgiving song. Most people were going to need other types of language after their laments.

3. Leviticus

If we were among the "lucky" few who needed to pay special attention to laws regarding thanksgiving sacrifice, as time passes, we may continue to express our gratitude, but at some juncture the language becomes stale and less fitting. At the same time it becomes more and more difficult to work ourselves up into an intense frame of mind to express "genuine thanks" to God like we did the first time. I meet a lot of students who carry backpacks loaded with guilt because they don't feel as excited about their conversion or some other big event as when it first occurred.

This problem stems from a basic misunderstanding of thanksgiving and the Psalms. First, thanksgiving is not meant to last forever. Like lament, thanksgiving is a transitory mode of speech intended for specific moments in the life of a believer and the community. Second, as time passes and the believer grows her language will naturally develop into new dialects such as assurance, confidence, or perhaps even teaching others to rely on God based on her experience. There is no need to work myself up into an inauthentic performance just to show I am still grateful. After all, presenting strange fire to the LORD is a risky business—just ask Nadab and Abihu (Lev 10).

4. Numbers

Thanksgiving psalms do not locate us or take us back to the same place we were with God before the crisis. Despite their failures in the wilderness, Moses did not take the Israelites back to Sinai every time they failed in the Book of Numbers. That would indeed seem strange. But why do the Psalms not save a few columns on the scroll and take us back to the praises we sang before anything happened? Because these writers and editors understand the life of faith: 1) If the crisis was deep enough to solicit lament, then after God's rescue the place we once occupied with God no longer exists, in part because 2) the experience has changed us. We can only pick up from where we are now and move forward from this point with our lives and our relationship with God. And to do this we need new languages to facilitate the relationship—as it is now, not as it used to be.

5. Deuteronomy

Just as with the selection of laments in chapter three, the selection of psalms that come after lament and the category to which they belong is a subjective decision. The individual psalms do not present themselves in precise types for the benefit of my thesis. Instead, the psalms overlap with their ideas, patterns, and vocabulary. For example, every writer I know regards Psalm 30 to be a psalm of thanksgiving (including myself). And yet, the psalmist only uses the word "thanks" two times (30:4b, 12b), while primarily using the vocabulary of praise: "I will extol you, O LORD" (30:1a), "Sing praises to the LORD, O you his faithful ones" (30:4a), and "you have taken off my sackcloth and clothed me with joy so that my soul may praise you and not be silent" (30:11b, 12a). Or, to take a second example, Psalm 136 (a miniature Deuteronomy, retelling Israel's exodus and conquest of the Transjordan) is loaded with the vocabulary of a thanksgiving psalm: "O give thanks to the LORD. . . O give thanks to the God of gods. . . O give thanks to the LORD of LORDS" (136:1a, 2a, 3a), and "O give thanks to the God of heaven" (136:26a). The psalm also celebrates a recent unspecified victory (136:23a, 24a). Thus, I categorize Psalm 136 as a thanksgiving song—but this time I go against most of my colleagues who take this psalm to be a hymn of praise. (So Limburg 462–463, and Clifford 268–269; Gerstenberger (388) considers Psalm 136 to be a communal hymn of thanksgiving).

Psalms of Thanksgiving

1. The Form of Thanksgiving

In order to carry its principle ideas the form of a thanksgiving psalm typically consists of four common elements. Psalm 30 is a tried and true example because here the four elements appear in a "pure state" and in an order that avoids confusing overlap. Consequently we are able to see what the writers of thanksgiving are working with before we get to more complex texts.

A. In Psalm 30 the first building block is *an initial outburst of gratitude*, words that cannot be held back a second longer—like the sudden and fierce embrace of lovers in an airport or a hometown crowd standing to cheer a game-winning goal.

> I will extol you, O LORD, for you have drawn me up,
>   and did not let my foes rejoice over me.
> O LORD my God, I cried to you for help,
>   and you have healed me.
> O LORD, you brought my soul from Sheol,
>   restored me to life from among those gone down to
>   the Pit. (30:1–3)

As an introduction, these initial lines are peppered with clues as to what has happened and who is responsible, all within a three-part movement from them (third person) to me (first person), to you (second person):

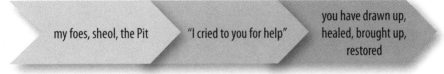

This movement emphasizes one of the key themes of thanksgiving psalms: what has brought about the change from lament to new life is nothing other than God and nothing less than an act of God. Things did not just "work out" or "get better" (my own flawed language); nor did we, despite our advanced knowledge, heal the sick, save the marriage, or harvest a bumper crop. Look again at how often in the first three verses the writer uses the words God, LORD, or you (referring to God) as the subject of an action verb (I have included instances in which the NRSV holds back on the term "you" [present in the Hebrew] to spare us the redundancy).

> ***you*** have drawn me up
> {***you***} did not let my foes rejoice
> ***you*** have healed me
> ***O LORD***, you brought my soul from Sheol
> {***you***} restored me to life

God and God alone is responsible for the change, the movement from illness to health, from conflict to peace, and from death to life. The trouble did not just get better, arrive at a peace agreement, or resolve itself—as if God had nothing to do with the outcome. Instead, as we are prone to forget or too timid to claim, this psalmist cannot imagine anything "getting better" without God.

B. In the second element, the psalmist *extends an invitation to others to join the proclamation of thanks.*

> Sing praises to the LORD, O you his faithful ones,
>   and give thanks to his holy name.
> For his anger is but for a moment;
>   his favor is for a lifetime.
> Weeping may linger for the night,
>   but joy comes with the morning. (30:4–5)

Just as lament was a public affair, so must thanksgiving be a matter of public record that includes other voices. The psalmist urges others to become a part of the celebration for at least two reasons: First, thanksgiving is good news to share, joy that I cannot keep to myself; I must tell others. Once upon a time I played golf. And one fine day with a slight wind in my face and the pin (hole) 135 yards away, my eight iron and I combined to hit the perfect shot—a hole in one! (And yes, I have witnesses who signed the score card.) The celebration began there and continued with phone calls as soon as I got home (in the age before cell phones). More important, "news of an engagement" cannot wait until the morning; or do you recall your response to the surprise picture of your first grandchild, so tiny and in utero, but creating good news that must be shared. Second, alone I am unable to give sufficient, appropriate thanks. I need your help now, just as I needed your help in lament. This is the spirit of annual awards at school or a business; it's one thing for the boss to tell you that you are doing a great job, but a different matter to be recognized for your work by all of your colleagues at a company event.

These verses introduce another common theme of these psalms: thanksgiving speaks the truth, the whole truth—without a public relations agent holding us back or spinning the truth until it is distorted beyond recognition. God is love; and God has an explosive temper (5a; cf. Exod 32:10, 33:3, 34:6–7). So life with this God sometimes includes weeping through the night (5). Thanksgiving does not cover-up or deny the pain we have experienced.

C. The heart of thanksgiving is *retelling our story*, what happened to bring us to this point of gratitude:

> As for me, I said in my prosperity,
> "I shall never be moved."
> By your favor, O LORD,
> you had established me as a strong mountain;
> you hid your face;
> I was dismayed.
> To you, O LORD, I cried,
> and to the LORD I made supplications:
> "What profit is there in my death,
> if I go down to the Pit?
> Will the dust praise you?
> Will it tell of your faithfulness?
> Hear, O LORD, and be gracious to me!
> O LORD, be my helper!"
> You have turned my mourning into dancing;
> you have taken off my sackcloth
> and covered me with joy, (30:6–11)

Like a teenager who regards himself as invincible or Job offering his morning sacrifice, or a believer seduced by a gospel of health and wealth, this psalmist thought he had the LORD's stamp of approval: "established as a strong mountain" (7a). But then, for no apparent reason, God looked away; he "hid" his face (7b). In the priestly blessing of Numbers 6 the direction God looks is critical: May the LORD "make his face to shine upon you" (Num 6:25), may "the LORD lift up his countenance upon you" (Num 6:26). If God looks our direction we may expect grace (25) and peace (26)—complete fullness of life. But when God hides his face, life turns into hell on earth; the psalmist is not merely "dismayed" (NRSV) but terrified or horrified. The strong mountain crumbles into dust.

Remarkably, this psalmist remembers or still has access to his former lament and now uses that lament (vv 9–10) as part of the thanksgiving hymn. In his lament, he had argued that his death (literal or a metaphoric "living death") would serve no purpose. If left in this condition or allowed to die, he will not be able to tell about God's faithfulness (9). Neither his death (as he understands the afterlife) nor "living death" will permit him to talk about God. He cannot pretend all is well and sing the songs of praise when God's face is turned away; these words of lament correspond to what many have shared with me about times in their lives in which they could not sing. How does one sing gratitude after the loss of a spouse, during (and after) a divorce, or some other life-changing event without forfeiting integrity? Unfortunately, however, the poet's practice runs counter to the custom of many churches that urge their members to get over grief quickly and leave troubles outside the church doors so that we may offer genuine praise. From the Psalms, such a thing is impossible; no one can be two places at one time—no one can leave part of life outside communion with God.

As the psalmist testifies, his earlier lament worked; he prayed that God would save him from death and God did. God changed his clothes, removing the sackcloth of mourning and clothing him with joy; God also changes the funeral that was to mourn his death into a dance celebrating new life! A party unlike any he has ever seen—unbridled joy meets unrestrained celebration—all because God answered this prayer of lament.

D. The last common element of a thanksgiving psalm is a statement of consequence: what now? What will we do with our lives in response to what God has done for us? Our psalmist promises praise and everlasting thanksgiving:

So that my soul may praise you and not be silent.
O Lord my God, I will give thanks to you forever.
(30:12)

As long as I live (forever), I will tell people what you (God) have done for my life (12a). I will not and cannot be silent. Just as I had to speak in lament, now I must speak in gratitude.

So then, psalms of thanksgiving are composed of these four basic elements: a) an initial exuberant outburst of gratitude, b) an invitation for others to join the celebration, c) retelling one's story from the onset of trouble until resolution in new life, and last, d) a declaration of what one will do in the future for God.

2. The Joy of Victory: Enemies in Thanksgiving Songs

Like artists using different colors of paste, Hebrew poets not only play with the order and placement of the elements of thanksgiving, they experiment with textures and shapes in remarkably different ways. For example, **Psalm 124** can hardly get beyond its own astonishment of what God has just done. It's one of those times that you say, "No one is going to believe this." And they won't, because you had to be there—and even then, oh how this God can still surprise just when you least expect it. The proclamation needs a witness; "let Israel now say" (124:1) or no one will ever believe it, not even Israel. But what surprised the psalmist (and the community) is buried deep beneath the writer's abstract art of metaphor and simile.

Sometimes the only way to tell the truth is with head-spinning, mind-blowing images, one stacked upon the other (just ask John of the Revelations). So in Psalm 124, for us to hear the central feature of thanksgiving, retelling the story, is to enter a world far, far away. a) An *enemy* attacked like the ancient death god *Mot*, opening his jaws to swallow us alive, death only moments away (3). b) The waters of chaos (another familiar ancient Near Eastern image) broke through limits assigned by God, knocking us off our feet, sweeping us downstream, catching us in the undertow, pulling us down, and choking us in the raging waters (3–5). c) We were also the prey to wild animals chasing us; running, out of breath, death only a matter of seconds away (6). d) Finally, we were the hunter's prey, a bird caught in a trap; every move we made just got us stuck worse, and we have only minutes to live until the hunter makes his rounds (7).

But marvel of marvels, you are not going to believe this; we can hardly believe it ourselves—and we were there. God broke the trap, God gave us speed to outrun the cheetah, God pulled the plug on the chaos-water, and then God propped open *Mot's* jaws (death) with a stick and we all walked out. Unbelievable? Absolutely! Crazy talk? You know it. But did it happen? Oh yes. "Our help is in the name of the LORD, who made heaven and earth" (124:8). Oddly enough, however, with all the imagery in Psalm 124 we have little idea of what actually happened to prompt this outburst of gratitude. We know that there was an enemy of some sort, most likely another nation or group; and this enemy attacked, perhaps a military assault. But the identity of the enemy, whoever or whatever they may be and whatever the attack may represent, is not provided by this psalm.

The enemy is also a feature of **Psalm 92**. More in common with standard psalms of thanksgiving than Psalm 124, Psalm 92 begins with an initial outburst of gratitude (92:1–3) that includes a brief synopsis of what happened: "For you, O LORD, have made me glad by your work; at the works of your hands I sing for joy" (92:4). But just what "work" the LORD has been up to, to deserve such praise is at best ambiguous; we have no idea what has happened. In his retelling of events (6–11), with awe the poet considers the LORD's works and thoughts (5), subjects beyond the grasp of the dullard and stupid (6): despite appearances, though it may seem that the LORD permits the wicked to "sprout like grass" and "flourish," in fact "they are doomed to destruction forever" (7). The poet identifies these people ("all evil doers") as enemies of the LORD ("your enemies who shall perish" [8]). In contrast, the LORD has "exalted my horn" like a wild ox that gores and kills (10, "horn" here is a symbol of power and strength). So I have seen "the downfall of my enemies" and heard their doom (11).

It is difficult in this psalm not to identify the LORD's wicked enemies with the enemies of the psalmist. In fact, I think that is precisely the connection the poet wants us to make. The evil enemies of the LORD (9) are also the "evil assailants" of the psalmist (11); most likely real people who have opposed the psalmist in some way, but now are also identified as God's enemies.

Psalm 92 concludes (element four: "so what") with imagery similar to Psalm 1. In Psalm 1 the righteous "are like trees planted by streams of water, which yield their fruit in season" (1:3). In Psalm 92 the righteous grow and flourish like palms or cedars in Lebanon, but they are planted in the temple courts (92:12–13). Here, living in the presence of God, even in their old age they are full of sap and produce fruit (14)— proof of the psalmist's claims that the LORD is upright (15). In Psalm 1 the wicked are "like chaff that the wind drives away" (1:4); in Psalm 92 the evildoers that sprouted and flourished like grass (92:7) will also be scattered (92:9).

The motif of enemies also appears in other psalms of thanksgiving, two of which merit consideration here. **Psalm 138** closely follows the pattern set by Psalm 30. Verses 1–3 express exuberant thanks (1–2) with an abbreviated retelling of what happened (3). The typical call for others to join in the thanksgiving occurs in verses 4–6 with a twist; here the psalmist does not need to invite others because "All the kings of the earth *shall* praise you, O LORD, for *they have heard* the words of your mouth" (4, emphasis mine). Their praise is already assured because they have heard that "though the LORD is high, he regards the lowly" (6a) and this knowledge will bring them to join the singer in praising the LORD.

In an unusual move, Psalm 138 does not include the story of God's rescue. Instead, a statement of confidence fills this role: "Though I walk in the midst of trouble, you preserve me against the wrath of my *enemies*; you stretch out your hand, and your right hand delivers me" (7, emphasis mine). The story is not over yet; angry enemies still surround the writer. But though danger is still present, the psalmist is confident that God still protects him. The psalm concludes with the final movement of thanksgiving psalms: consequence (what I will do now). Here, however, because the danger still exists, the poet concludes with more confidence that "the LORD will fulfill his purposes for me" and asks the LORD, "Do not forsake the work of your hands" (8). Again, the enemies that surround and threaten the psalmist are unknown. A mask of secrecy shields their identity.

A second thanksgiving psalm with the motif of enemies that merits our special consideration is **Psalm 136**. Poetically, Psalm 136 is an unusual psalm; it is written as an antiphonal call and response song. Someone sings or chants the first line of each verse and a chorus or second group responds with the second line of each verse: "for his steadfast love endures forever." The first three verses call the congregation to thanksgiving and the fourth verse sets the theme of the psalm: "who [God] alone does great wonders." The psalm includes such great wonders as creation (5–9), the exodus (10–16), and conquest of land east of the Jordan (17–22). Then the language changes from third person "them" to first person "us," and the topic of thanksgiving moves from the distant past to a recent event in which God "rescued *us* from *our* foes" (24, emphasis mine). But once again, we have no hard evidence as to the identity of the enemy. The prior verse only mentions that God "remembered us in our low estate" (23). The enemies escape again into the darkness of ambiguity. Or do they?

The enemy was a common figure in the laments, appearing in over 40 of the 60 chapters of lament (*Hurting with God*, 247–249). These enemies either caused the trouble or made the most of opportunities to take advantage of those already hurting. Consequently, the key for resolving a lament often relied on settling the problem of the enemy. So it should come as no surprise that this same ambiguous figure materializes in the songs of thanksgiving. At times the enemy appears to be a real person—a political rival, foreign king(s), or other nations (e.g., Ps 92 and 124). At other times the enemy is more vague;

it could be anything that stands against the life or well-being of the psalmist (e.g., Ps 136, 138). Historically, such ambiguity is frustrating; why didn't the poet identify his or her antagonists so that we could understand these psalms better? But from a literary-theological viewpoint, the ambiguity of these psalms is the genius of the writers and perhaps the greatest gift of the psalms to the reader. As we read, the enemy may become anything or anyone—whatever we are facing or that stands against our lives; all we know is what we are able to imagine with the writer, and that is "if it had not been the LORD who was on our side" the attack—the audit, the biopsy, the slide into head-on traffic, the fire, or the heart attack—would have had a different ending. Indeed, it is "good to give thanks to the LORD, to sing praises to your name, O Most High" (92:1).

3. Let the Redeemed of the LORD Say So

While Psalms 92, 124, 136, and 138 each give thanks for escape from an enemy, **Psalm 107** issues a summons to those redeemed by the LORD to "say so" (107:2a). Or as the poet states in the opening lines, "give thanks to the LORD, for he is good; for his steadfast love endures forever" (1). Four vignettes follow that test the limits of the LORD's goodness and his ability to redeem. Each tale follows the same pattern, beginning with a description of the trouble: people lost and dying in the desert (4–5), prisoners in gloom, broken by hard labor (10–12), sick persons coming close to death (17–18), and sailors caught in a vicious storm at sea (23–27). Then, the writer states, in all four stories "they cried to the LORD in their trouble, and he delivered them from their distress" (6, 13, 19, 28): God led those lost in the desert to an inhabited town (7), God led the prisoners out of the gloom and broke their chains (14), God healed the sick (20), and God calmed the storm and brought the weary sailors to their desired port (30). Next, in all four stories, the poet encourages each group with the same words: "Let them thank the LORD for his steadfast love, for his wonderful works to humankind" (8, 15, 21, 31). Finally, two of the vignettes conclude with another reason why those in each story should give thanks to the LORD: because "he satisfies the thirsty" and fills the hungry (9), and because he shatters prison doors and cuts bars of iron (16). The other two stories emphasize the need for a thanksgiving sacrifice (22) or praise in the congregation (32).

The final words of the psalm (33–43) allude to a fifth and even sixth episode of God's redemptive ability. The fifth episode is the Exodus (33–38): providing water in the wilderness (33–35), giving land in which the redeemed plant crops, establish villages, and "By his blessing they multiply greatly" (38a, cf. Gen 12:2, 13:16, 15:5, 17:6). Finally, the sixth episode is the present context of exile in which those who multiplied greatly are diminished and brought low (39). Here too, however, the Lord goes to work. On one side, he exiles princes and makes them wander in the wilderness (40). On the other side, he raises those in need (Israel) out of distress and makes their families like flocks that he will lead home (?) or bless with fertility (?) or both. Thus, the Psalm concludes, let the wise discern what the LORD is about to do for his people (43).

The placement of Psalm 107 in the Book of Psalms also suggests a reading of the final verses (39–43) or the entire psalm as anticipation of a return from exile. The last verse in the preceding psalm (discounting the editorial doxology in verse 48) begs the LORD to save us "and gather us from among the nations, that we may give thanks to your holy name and glory in your praise" (106:47). With these words Book Four of the Psalter comes to a close. Then, with Psalm 107, the fifth and final book begins with the words:

> Let the redeemed of the LORD say so,
> those he redeemed from trouble
> and gathered in from the lands,
> from the east and from the west,
> from the north and from the south. (107:2–3)

Viewed within this literary context, each of the vignettes of rescue are representative, not exhaustive, of the kinds of things the LORD is doing to gather his people back to himself and to the land—actions which merit all of Israel declaring, "O give thanks to the LORD, for he is good; for his steadfast love endures forever" (107:1).

4. Up in Smoke and Out of Date?

A good many Christians wince at the mention of sacrifice and are quick-draw specialists in anti-sacrificial rhetoric in both Hebrew and Greek texts. To summarize: we don't do "sacrifice" because Jesus offered himself as a once-for-all-time sacrifice (Hebrews 7, 9–10) and so brought to an end a bloody, disgusting, barbaric, and ineffective religious practice (my pen quivers at all of the misunderstanding of sacrifice packed into one sentence, but that's a book for another time). Most research concludes that psalms of thanksgiving were developed to accompany thanksgiving sacrifices, at least as long as the tabernacle or temple was present and functioning. When the temple was not available, e.g., after the Babylonian conquest (2 Kgs 25:8–9) until Zerubbabel's return (Ezra 1:1–4, 3:1–3), a "spiritualization" of the psalms occurred in which the thanksgiving psalm took the place of the sacrifice (thus, perhaps, the anti-sacrificial attitude in Ps 40:6–7 and 51:15–17).

Among the psalms we have examined so far in this chapter, only Psalm 107 mentions sacrifice. Here the writer encouraged those whom the LORD healed to "offer thanksgiving sacrifices, and tell of his deeds with songs of joy" (107:22). Other psalms of thanksgiving also refer to sacrifices and vows. Psalm 118 celebrates an unlikely victory, and gives thanks to the LORD: "this is the LORD's doing; it is marvelous in our eyes" (118:23). The psalm describes a processional that leads to the temple where the psalmist instructs someone to "Bind the festal procession with branches, up on the horns of the altar" (118:27b). As translated, the text suggests that a sacrifice is tied onto the altar. This understanding of the text, however, is debated among interpreters (see Zenger, *Psalms 3*, 243).

Psalms that we will consider in later chapters also mention vows and/or sacrifices. Psalm 65 begins by mentioning "to you shall vows be performed" (65:1). Psalm 66 speaks at length about vows and sacrifices.

> I will come into your house with burnt offerings;
>> I will pay you my vows.
> Those that my lips uttered
>> and my mouth promised when I was in trouble.
> I will offer to you burnt offerings of fatlings,
>> with the smoke of the sacrifice of rams;
> I will make an offering of bulls and goats. (66:13–15)

Here, it is clear that vows or promises were made when the psalmist was in trouble; if God would help him, then he would offer sacrifices and keep other vows. We often see such promises in the laments (e.g., 22:25, 35:9, 18, 43:4, 51:13, 15, 52:9, 54:6, 56:12–13, 61:5,8, 69:30–31, 79:13, 80:18, 109:30)

By far, **Psalm 116** provides the most extensive integration of psalm and sacrificial ritual in the Psalter. Early, the psalm includes familiar movements such as initial exuberant thanksgiving (1–2), a brief synopsis of what has happened (3–4), and a long ambiguous review of events with praise for God who made all the difference (5–11). Then the language becomes liturgical, leading us through a thanksgiving ceremony. The psalmist asks, "What shall I return to the LORD for all his bounty to me?" (12), and in response initiates the presentation of a drink offering (13–14) and a thanksgiving sacrifice (17–18).

Between lifting the "cup of salvation" and offering a "thanksgiving sacrifice" are two verses that are often misunderstood and misused. Many popular interpretations use 116:15 at funerals to assert that the death of a faithful person is a blessing to God: "Precious in the sight of the LORD is the death of his faithful servants" (NIV). In the context of Psalm 116, however, these two verses express the opposite idea. The potential death of the psalmist was not going to be a blessing to the LORD. Instead, the reason the psalmist did not die was because God could not bear the cost ("precious"—which carries the idea of costly) of his or her death; God would have lost a faithful servant and a voice of praise. And to read just a bit of Christian theology into the text: God has more than enough servants in heaven. He does not need another angel. What God needs are people who live out lives of service and trust on earth.

While rethinking atonement sacrifice in view of the Christ event, New Testament writers did not view thanksgiving sacrifice to be out of date, though they did continue the "spiritualization" of sacrifice already in process before and during the era of the second temple; they regarded the practice of praise (Heb 13:15), sharing with others (Heb 13:16), service (Philip 2:17), and the support of those proclaiming the gospel (Philip 4:18) to be acts of sacrifice. And, of course, Romans 12 asserts that we offer our own bodies as sacrifices to the LORD:

> I appeal to you therefore, brothers and sisters, by the mercies of God, to present your bodies as *a living sacrifice*, holy and acceptable to God, which is your spiritual worship. Do not be conformed to this world, but be transformed by the renewing of your minds, so that you may discern what is the will of God—what is good and acceptable and perfect. (Rom 12:1–3, emphasis mine)

I fear that the challenge for Christians is not the idea or even practice of thanksgiving; we do praise and worship with a level of professionalism that would knock the Levitical Temple Singers off their feet—all types of instruments, sound professionally mixed and amplified, multi-colored lights, television cameras, and super giant screen projection. I have no personal objection to any of these things, and more important, I don't think New Testament theology objects. Much of what we see in worship these days is the adaptation to culture that must take place wherever the church spreads. Our challenge is in the sacrifice—giving something of ourselves that really matters, costs, or is precious to us. We don't even have to buy a ticket to worship, but selling sacrifice is a tough business these days. We all would rather hear about the good life God has for us than the challenge of picking up a cross to follow Jesus.

Three Conclusions

1. The direction in which lament leads us is ultimately *not* up to us. We may struggle against our enemies with all our strength and ingenuity, and pray with all our might. But we do not control the outcome. At Twelve-Step programs, including pain management programs, we must first confess that we are powerless over our enemy—whatever it may be: alcohol, food, drugs, work, or pain. So what this means is that if anything has gotten better, we can be sure that it was not our power, ingenuity, or goodness that did it—only grace. God's grace. Just as thanksgiving psalms attribute deliverance to no one other than God (e.g., 30:1–3), genuine thanksgiving today is about God and only God.

At its heart, thanksgiving is a matter of telling (and retelling) the stories of how God broke into our lives to provide what we most needed, but least expected:

> an anonymous check for $2,000 that kept me from dropping out of my Ph.D. program and kept me in school
> *Thank You, Lord*

> the friends and churches on site the morning after my house burned when we had nothing that was not chargrilled or smoked
> *Thank You, Lord*

> whoever it was that took my children shopping for new clothes that morning
> *Thank You, Lord*

> that my son had just changed places to ride shot-gun in the lead van a few miles before the trailing van flipped and rolled off the highway
> *Thank You, Lord*

No one died
Thank You, Lord

for those who rallied around me as the pain of divorce and the
pain in my feet and legs became unbearable
Thank You, Lord

You too, my friend, have stories to tell. Find a way to tell them and so
thank God.

2. This definition of thanksgiving helps makes sense of the non-
sense that confuses so many believers every Sunday. If thanksgiving—in
the Psalms and most any dictionary—denotes the expression of gratitude for some specific act, then singing "thanksgiving songs" that lack a
narrative (story) or that we do not preface with a reason to give thanks
confuses and leaves believers beating themselves up for not feeling as
grateful as they should, or struggling to get 'jazzed up' in order to give
thanks. At the heart of thanksgiving is a story, something happening
in the life of a believer. Once we are equipped with a story we will have
no struggle to get in the right frame of mind; we will be eager to join
in the celebration.

3. I would prefer closing this chapter without bringing up one final
practical difficulty. How are we to express thanksgiving for God sparing my child riding on one van when those on the second van were
seriously injured? This is especially difficult in churches that do what I
have advocated here; they tell the stories of those in the church whom
God has blessed with healing, bringing them to the front, applauding
God, and praying thanksgiving. But what about me? The pain in my
legs is no less now than it was when I came into the auditorium in my
wheelchair. More important, what about the mother holding her son
who has leukemia and who will not get better? He died before this book
was completed. How do we express thanks to God for one child while
the other child dies? How do we not add to what is already massive
pain? I don't have all the answers, but I do know that we must begin
with honesty: expressing our gratitude to the LORD with exuberance

and making space to cry out over our losses, even recognizing those who are living out faith despite God's answer, "No."

CHAPTER SIX

Spoke #3: Singing a New Hallelujah

Hannah was a remarkable woman caught in heartrending circumstances. She was married to a man who loved her (1 Sam 1:5), even if he didn't grasp the danger of her situation. Hannah was barren in a world that not only valued women for their ability to produce children but relied on those children to care for and protect their parents later in life. Without a child, especially a male, Hannah knows that if her husband dies before her, she will become part of the other biblical trinity: widows, orphans, and aliens—who live on the charity and good will of the community, which oftentimes is no life at all. Elkanah, her husband, doesn't seem to grasp her situation when he tries to comfort Hannah by turning her attention to his love for her: "Am I not more to you than ten sons?" (1:8). What he doesn't understand is that the issue is not his love, but *her future*. No, Elkanah, this time you are not more to Hannah than ten sons.

Possibly because of Hannah's inability to bear children, Elkanah has a second wife who is a veritable baby-producing machine. And this wife, Peninnah, has all the charm of a middle school snot who loves to jerk Hannah's chain. "So it's Mother's Day again? Let's see, Hannah where do you think we should go to celebrate? Oh, so sorry—I keep forgetting that you don't have any children." The text describes Hannah's situation: "her rival used to provoke her severely, to irritate her, because the LORD had closed her womb" (1:6). Nothing like a humiliating problem, a threat to your future well-being, a husband who doesn't understand, a rival who loves to rub it in your face, all to go along with the theological premise: even God is against Hannah. Year after year after year.

One year during the family's annual trip to Shiloh, the central religious meeting place before Jerusalem, Hannah could take no more. As soon as the party was over, she bolted for the tabernacle (or temple, 2 Sam 1:9) and the presence of God where, with tears, she lays her life before the LORD:

> O LORD of hosts, if only you will look on the misery of your
> servant, and remember me and not forget your servant, but
> will give to your servant a male child, then I will set him
> before you as a Nazirite until the day of his death. He shall
> drink neither wine nor intoxicants, and no razor shall touch
> his head. (1 Sam 1:11)

Another man in the story, the priest Eli, also doesn't understand Hannah or the situation; he observes her lips moving with no sound and accuses her of making a drunken spectacle of herself (1:13–14). Last year, even the year before she might have taken the fall for the priest's error, but not this year; tonight Hannah defends herself: I've not been drinking but pouring out my life to the LORD—a life filled with trouble and anxiety (1:15–16). And tonight, with her unapologetic lament, Hannah's life begins to change. Apparently without knowing the content of her prayer, Eli speaks an "oracle of salvation": "Go in peace; the God of Israel grant the petition you have made to him" (1:17).

Hannah's story is a silent plague among us: women who desperately want a baby in their arms but who cannot get pregnant, or who finally become pregnant only to miscarry the pregnancy. Or mothers and fathers who somehow live through the burial of their child. I have no words for these parents, and no heart to suggest that they praise God. If you do, let me know and give me some time until I can go with you and superglue your mouth shut. There is a time to be silent (Eccles 3:7).

To be fair to the Almighty, the second half of Hannah's story also surrounds us. Fast-forward five or more years into the future and Hannah is back at the tabernacle in Shiloh, her first trip back since giving birth to a son (1:19–23). She has returned this day to keep the vow that she made in her lament: to devote her son to the LORD's service for as long as he lives (1:22, 27–28). And this year her words to the LORD are transformed from lament to praise. She prays/sings a psalm that is probably not her own composition, but a song she knows will express her feelings toward God.

> My heart exults in the LORD;
>> my strength is exalted in my God.
> My mouth derides my enemies,
>> because I rejoice in my victory.
>
> Those who were full have hired themselves out for bread,
>> but those who were hungry are fat with spoil.
> *The barren has borne seven,*
>> *but she who has many children is forlorn.*
>
> The LORD makes poor and makes rich;
>> he brings low, he also exalts.
> He raises up the poor from the dust;
>> he lifts the needy from the ash heap,
> to make them sit with princes
>> and inherit a seat of honor. (1 Sam 2:1, 5, 7–8,
>> emphasis mine)

With Hannah the LORD has worked another of his famous reversals of fortune; the barren is no longer barren, the needy have left the ash heap, and the poor no longer grovel in the dust (2:8). And so Hannah sings—what else can she do? What else can any of us do when the LORD does something that changes everything? Moses (Exod 15:1–18) and Miriam (15:20–21) sang on the other side of the sea, with Pharaoh's troops cut down by the water. Deborah sang when the LORD crushed the enemy and returned *Shalom*—peace and fullness of life—to Israel (Judg 5:1–31). As we will soon see, the Psalms provide many new praises for God's people to use when God does it again—bringing new life out of death.

Before we leave Hannah standing in the tabernacle singing her song (yes, a woman singing solo in the tabernacle), more needs to be said about this woman, her sacrifice, and her song. The text is quick to point out that once Hannah leaves her son at the tabernacle, the LORD takes notice of her and grants her three more sons and two daughters—just as it reminds us that Samuel grows up "in the presence of the LORD" (1 Sam 2:21). We know that Hannah is going to have other children, but she doesn't. On this day, while she sings her song she leaves her only child to grow up miles from home, so far away that she will see him only once a year. Each year she will make him a "little robe" and take it to him during the annual trip to Shiloh (2:19). So every year she will have to guess how much her firstborn son has grown. I can't imagine that pain. I do wonder if Samuel understood why he did not grow up at home, how he must have cried for his mother and father that day—and many more; I wonder if he knew how much his mother loved him, if he knew how often his mother cried for him. You may accuse me of reading too much into the text, but I cannot imagine Hannah singing that day in Shiloh without seeing the tears running down her face for the sacrifice she is about to make—as she turns and leaves her son with strangers.

I don't know how Hannah can praise God with such apparent ease. The Sunday after our house fire I stood with tears singing (or trying to sing) "I Stand in Awe of You": "You are beautiful beyond description, too marvelous for words." Ten years later, when I was going through a divorce, I could not sing about God's work in the world or even God's goodness. My world was not settled or stable, but torn and utterly empty. Those were weeks and months of lament, which meant silence at most every church assembly. Somewhere along the line we confused the text, "Rejoice with those who rejoice and weep with those who weep," to say "Rejoice with those who rejoice and ignore those who weep." But that's a different book; see *Hurting with God* (ACU Press, 2012).

For those of us whose laments have not led to the response we wanted from God, it seems clear enough that neither continued lament nor thanksgiving is the language we need. But neither does the language of new praise make any sense; after all, if thanksgiving is a pat on the back for a job well done, praise is a red carpet celebration in honor of God's work. Pardon me, but it is difficult for me to imagine singing new praise when my pain is elevated and my medicine ineffective. And yet there are those psalms that are determined to praise the LORD regardless of the circumstances.

Learning to Sing Again: Psalm Genres Leading to Praise

To discover how the Book of Psalms leads us from lament to praise, in the first half of this chapter I explore the movement toward praise within other genres (lament and thanksgiving), as well as the appropriateness of certain old praises for those in and out of lament. I then examine the presence of new praises in the Psalter that possess all the traits of the hymns or praise psalms and a keen awareness of time spent in throes of lament. Finally, in the second half of the chapter I will consider the gains of contemporary scholarship over the past forty years as it follows the movement from lament to praise within the Book of Psalms. What we will discover along these two distinct trails may help us understand how Hannah, and others like her are able to sing praise in the midst of pain.

1. Laments Leading to Praise

Among the laments discussed in chapter three we found several psalms that led or encouraged their readers toward praise, the third spoke on the wagon wheel. Looking back, on the one hand, some writers of lament want to praise the LORD, but find some obstacle beyond their control blocking their path to the place of worship (Jerusalem?):

> My soul thirsts for God,
>> for the living God.
> When shall I come and behold
>> the face of God?
>
> These things I remember,
>> as I pour out my soul:
> How I went with the throng,
>> and led them in procession to the house of God
> with glad shouts and songs of thanksgiving,
>> a multitude keeping festival.
> Why are you cast down, O my soul,
>> and why are you disquieted within me?
> Hope in God; for I shall again praise him,
>> my help and my God. (42:2,4-6a)

On the up side, once the barrier that is causing this writer's exile from the presence of God is cleared, he will again go to God's dwelling place in joyful worship (43:3–4). On the down side, until that time comes the writer is helpless to change his circumstances and praise his God. In essence, God's worship depends on God's own actions to clear a path to praise.

On the other hand, sometimes lament writers are determined to praise the LORD despite difficult circumstances, even if God has not yet begun to work on their behalf—and may never do so. For example, in Psalm 59 the writer is facing enemies (perhaps nations, v. 5) who lay in ambush for his life (59:1–4). Every evening they come back like a pack of dogs on the prowl for food, demanding their fill or else (6–7, 14–15). Even so, though the LORD has not yet begun to save him, the poet praises God in the final two verses of the psalm:

> But I will sing of your might;

> I will sing aloud of your steadfast love in the morning.
> For you have been a fortress for me
> > and a refuge in the day of my distress.
> O my strength, I will sing praises to you,
> > for you, O God, are my fortress,
> > the God who shows me steadfast love. (59:16–17)

Though difficult for me to imagine, this psalmist is an example of a person who rises above the circumstances to exalt the LORD no matter what the present or future may hold.

2. *Thanksgiving Songs Leading to Praise*

As we have seen, thanksgiving focuses on a recent act of deliverance or help. Thus, thanksgiving psalms from chapter five spotlighted specific crises and God's intervention to save: attacks by enemies (Pss 92, 124, 136, 138), people lost in the desert (107:4–9), prisoners broken by hard labor (107:10–16), sick persons coming close to death (107:17–22), and sailors caught in a violent storm at sea (107:23–32). Generally speaking, these predicaments and the need for God's help are one-time events—as is the thanksgiving that follows God's rescue. Consequently, some of these psalms are content to give thanks without a concern to lead the reader to further praise.

Other thanksgiving psalms, however, naturally lead their readers toward more sustained gratitude expressed in praise. For example, Psalm 138 expresses thanksgiving for the day on which the LORD answered the poet's call for help (138:3). From this event the poet envisions his or her thanksgiving growing into praise from all the kings of the earth, because they hear the LORD's word and recognize that "though the LORD is high, he regards the lowly" (138:4–6): "All the kings of the earth shall praise you, O LORD" (138:4a). The typical pattern of thanksgiving psalms also leads the reader to a final expression of confidence in the LORD or a commitment to praise the LORD. Thus, Psalm 18 concludes,

> For this I will extol you, O LORD, among the nations,
>> and sing praises to your name.
> Great triumphs he gives to his king,
>> and shows steadfast love to his anointed,
>>> to David and his descendants forever. (18:49–50, cf. 2 Sam 22:50–51)

In a similar way, Psalm 30 leads the reader to praise:

> You have turned my mourning into dancing;
>> you have taken off my sackcloth
>> and covered me with joy,
> so that my soul may praise you and not be silent.
> O LORD my God, I will give thanks to you forever. (30:12)

In these psalms, God's help has changed everything and can never be forgotten. Consequently, the movement toward praise might be regarded as repeated thanksgiving for how God has broken into my life and saved me. So while some psalms of thanksgiving are adequate for a (one time) need, others lead to a more sustained praise.

3. The Continued Relevance of "Old Praise"

Unlike thanksgiving, the old praise psalms or hymns of orientation (as Brueggemann calls them) do not focus on a single event but "express a confident, serene settlement of faith issues. . . . they are statements that describe a happy, blessed state in which the speakers are grateful for and confident in the abiding, reliable gifts of life that are long-standing from time past and will endure for time to come" (*Message of the Psalms*, 25). These psalms, often referred to as hymns, reach back into history to remind us of a) God's power to save and b) what the past events reveal about God's character. Three examples will suffice.

1. In **Psalm 8**, the first hymn of praise in the Psalter, the writer marvels at two mysteries: a) God's glory exceeds the heavens, but is best chanted by infants (8:1–2), and b) in view of God's glory, demonstrated by the vastness of creation, why would God care so much for humans

to set us in charge of what God has made? Why would one so high and glorious give such honor to those so small? (8:3–9; cf Gen 1:26) But God has in fact given us dominion, the right to tend, care for, and reap; but as God's stewards, not the right to exploit and destroy. Indeed, as the psalm begins and ends, "O LORD, our Sovereign, how majestic is your name in all the earth!"

2. **Psalm 100** issues two summons to praise the LORD, each followed by reasons to praise (or the proclamation of the praise itself). First, verses 1–2 call the whole earth to "make a joyful noise," "worship the LORD with gladness," and enter "his presence with singing." Verse 3 gives reasons: Yahweh is God, he made us, so that we are his, "the sheep of his pasture." Curiously, here the writer seems to think everyone, not just Israel, is part of God's people (as is clear elsewhere, e.g., 117:1, 148:11–12). Second, in verse 4 the summons is to enter the temple compound with thanksgiving and praise, because "the LORD is good; his steadfast love endures forever, and his faithfulness to all generations" (v. 5). In his comments on this Psalm, James Mays points out that the liturgical role of Psalm 100 was a "processional song for movement through the gates of the temple into its courts (v. 4) where the LORD is present (v.2)" (*The Psalms*, 317). More important, however, Mays explains how this rather simple call to praise is in fact a call to make a decision about "the power to whom they entrust and submit their lives. . .the most significant social action a person can take" (*The Psalms*, 318).

3. In two sweeping movements **Psalm 148** issues a grand call for all things to praise the LORD. The first movement begins by summoning the heavenly beings (e.g., angels, 148:1–2) and heavenly creations (e.g., sun, moon, stars, 148:3–4) to praise the LORD not merely because the LORD created them, but because of their strength and durability (5–6). The second movement resumes the call to praise by summoning animate (e.g., animals, birds, people) and inanimate creations (e.g., fire, hail, snow, mountains) to praise the LORD by fulfilling his command (7–12, esp. v. 8). The final verses call people to praise: princes, kings, rulers, young and old, and male and female (11–12) because God's glory

outreaches creation itself (13), and finally, because God has raised a "horn" (a symbol of power, perhaps a king) for his people (14).

So while songs of thanksgiving celebrate specific and recent acts of deliverance, the hymns sing hallelujah on account of God's great acts in history (e.g., creation, the exodus) and because of God's nature or character as revealed by these historic events: the LORD is majestic in all the earth (8:1, 8), the LORD is good and "his steadfast love endures forever" (100:5), and "his name alone is exalted; his glory is above earth and heaven" (148:13). In other words, God's character and person supersede any particular current event. No matter what may happen or how bad things may become, these songs of praise hold out reasons for worshipping the LORD anyway, despite what God may or may not be doing at the present moment. Such praise is certainly no easy task.

When our worlds fall apart it is difficult to see beyond the pain in our lives to worship the LORD. For this reason I love Psalm 77, a lament with throbbing pain, crying out to the LORD with no answer (77:1).

> I think of God, and I moan;
>> I meditate, and my spirit faints. *Selah*
> You keep my eyelids from closing;
>> I am so troubled that I cannot speak. (77:2–3)

What the psalmist does in response, however, is counter-intuitive; instead of running from God, this writer determines to pull closer to God by remembering:

> I consider the days of old,
>> and remember the years of long ago...
> I will call to mind the deeds of the LORD;
>> I will remember your wonders of old.
> I will meditate on all your work,
>> and muse on your mighty deeds. (77:11–12)

We must remember who our God is, no matter how bad the day may be, even if the pain leaves me silent with my eyes closed, breathing with the pain. Without rushing to an easy fix, I can remember and affirm what those around me claim to be true in their songs. And I need their songs: "The steadfast love of the LORD never ceases," "Great is our God," "Hallelujah Praise Jehovah." I cannot ignore my own grappling with God, but neither can I deny these praises that will never change. Thus, we affirm another way in which those living in difficult circumstances may continue to praise the LORD.

4. New Praises

Some praises, however, may be even more suitable during and after our laments: the new praises admit to knowledge of life beyond "orientation" (when everything is wonderful and stable). Within their typical praise of God's reliability a number of psalms confess an awareness of the Pit and what God does for those sunk up to their neck in losses. Most often this confession is limited to just a few lines:

> For the LORD will vindicate his people,
>   and have compassion on his servants. (135:14)

> It is he who remembered us in our low estate,
>   for his steadfast love endures forever;
>   and rescued us from our foes,
>   for his steadfast love endures forever; (136:23–24)

> From the heavens you uttered judgment;
>   the earth feared and was still
> when God rose up to establish judgment,
>   to save all the oppressed of the earth. (76:8–9)

> Sing to God, sing praises to his name;
>   lift up a song to him who rides upon the clouds—
> his name is the LORD—
>   be exultant before him.
> Father of orphans and protector of widows
>   is God in his holy habitation.

> God gives the desolate a home to live in;
>> he leads out the prisoners to prosperity,
> but the rebellious live in a parched land. (Ps 68:4–6)

Each of these citations appears in what would otherwise be described as old praise or a hymn of orientation, but these writers know something else—something scandalous. They have lived long enough and been in the Pit enough times to know that praise for the great acts of the LORD in history and the person and character of the LORD is only part of the story. More must be said about how the LORD relates to those who do not experience life as a well-ordered gift of God. Three psalms especially merit a close examination.

1. **Psalm 103** issues an extended call to praise at its beginning (103:1–2) and end (103:20–22).

> Bless the LORD, O my soul,
>> and all that is within me,
> bless his holy name.
> Bless the LORD, O my soul,
>> and do not forget all his benefits—(103:1–2)

> Bless the LORD, O you his angels,
>> you mighty ones who do his bidding,
>> obedient to his spoken word.
> Bless the LORD, all his hosts,
>> his ministers that do his will.
> Bless the LORD, all his works
>> in all places of his dominion.
> Bless the LORD, O my soul. (103:20–22)

The initial summons to praise (bless = praise) leads us to the psalm's central idea: "do not forget *all his benefits*" (103:2, emphasis mine). In response, the psalmist recalls God's work among the outcasts of society:

> Who forgives all your iniquity,
>> who heals all your diseases,

> who redeems your life from the Pit,
>> who crowns you with steadfast love and mercy,
> who satisfies you with good as long as you live
>> so that your youth is renewed like the eagle's.
> The Lord works vindication
>> and justice for all who are oppressed. (103:3–6)

In the fashion of a praise psalm or hymn the writer describes God's benefits in a series of participles (e.g., "who forgives," "who heals"). But the content is unlike a typical hymn. The poet turns to the ancient traditions about Moses on Mount Sinai (103:7–10, cf. Exod 34:6–7) as well as other familiar traditions from Isaiah (103:5, cf. Isa 40:31; 103:9, cf. Isa 57:16; 103:11, cf. Isa 55:9, 103:15–16, cf. Isa 40:6–8; see Mays, *The Psalms*, 328) and Hosea (103:13, cf. Hos 11:1–7). But the hymn itself offers praise to the one who forgives because compassion and forgiveness are the Lord's basic nature (103:8–14), because he understands our basic nature (14–16), and because of his love for those who follow him (17–18). With such a scandalous Father on the loose, running around forgiving people, it is little wonder that the Son came forgiving sinners (Lk 7:36–50), eating with the wrong crowd (Mk 2:15–17), and touching the untouchables (Lk 4:12–15, 13:10–13).

2. **Psalm 113** also begins and ends with a call to worship ("Praise the Lord") and extends this call to all time (v. 2) and all places (v. 3) because God's glory is high above all nations and even the heavens (v. 4). At this point, the psalmist takes a left turn out of the right hand lane, catching us off guard.

> Who is like the Lord our God,
>> who is seated on high,
> who looks far down
>> on the heavens and the earth?
> He raises the poor from the dust
>> and lifts the needy from the ash heap,
> To make them sit with princes,

> with the princes of his people.
> He gives the barren woman a home,
>> making her the joyous mother of children.
> Praise the LORD! (113:5–9)

The writer speaks as one who has seen or even experienced the LORD's reversals: the poor and needy in the dust and ashes/ to sitting with princes; the barren/ to a joyous mother of children. (Hannah's song comes to mind at several points [1 Sam 2:5b, 7–8]). Beyond the classic acts in creation or in Israel's life, sustaining the status quo, this psalm celebrates a God who loves to help the helpless and turn things around for those headed in the wrong direction.

Like Psalm 103, it is not difficult to see how Psalm 113 flows out from the appeal on the spoke of lament that urges readers to praise God no matter what the present condition may be or what the future may hold. We praise a God who is worthy of praise (113:1–4) and a God who changes to match his own commitment to justice and fullness of life (113:5–9). We have no guarantee that what God has done for others he will do for us—that singing praise to a God who sets things right means that he will stop fooling around and do for us what he should have done weeks, months, or years ago. Nonetheless, what we see is that there are ways for us to do what the poets in the lament songs urge us to do: praise the LORD.

3. **Psalm 33** begins as a typical psalm of praise, issuing a summons to the upright to rejoice in the LORD (33:1), praising the LORD with a new song accompanied by the lyre, harp, and loud shouts (2–3). The initial cause for praise is also common to the hymns: a) the LORD's faithfulness, righteousness, justice, and steadfast love (4–5) and b) creation, described as the LORD gathering chaos waters "as in a bottle" (7) and speaking the world into existence.

> By the word of the LORD the heavens were made,
>> and all their host by the breath of his mouth. (6)

> For he spoke, and it came to be;
> he commanded, and it stood firm. (9)

At this point, however, the psalm leaves conventional references to the LORD's mighty works in the past to turn our attention to the LORD's contemporary work among the nations and those who fear him (10–19).

Similar to Psalm 113, the LORD looks down from heaven to watch all who live on the earth (13–15); what the LORD sees is that large armies, a warrior's brute strength, and the latest in military technology ("the war horse") are unable to secure victory (16–17). Investment in military power is weak counsel offered to kings over and over again. From where the LORD sits, he is able to watch all who fear him and who put their hope on his reliable love to save them from death and keep them alive in famine (most likely a reference to famine that comes as a result of military siege, 18–19). So, to backtrack to verses 10–11, the LORD thwarts the best-laid plans of kings and their many counselors because they rely on military strength, not the LORD. But the LORD's counsel stands forever, continually blessing his chosen people (10–12).

Victory, this poet realizes, does not depend on who has the most soldiers, the better-trained men, the best chariots, the better reconnaissance, or the best armored cavalry, planes and pilots, atomic powered submarines, destroyers, smart bombs, and dumb atomic bombs. What really matters for those beset by enemy invasions (of all types) is reliance on the LORD, who is "our help and shield" (20). We can relax with glad hearts because (and only because) we trust the LORD, not ourselves (21). So the psalm concludes:

> Let your steadfast love, O LORD, be upon us,
> even as we hope in you. (27)

Conclusion: Psalm 103, 113, and 33 come to us from human brokenness: sin (103), poverty and neediness (113), and war (33). And yet each psalm is a hymn that praises the LORD for how he steps into each situation to forgive, heal, and redeem from the Pit (103:3–4); raise the poor from the dust, lift the needy from the ash heap, and give the barren woman a home full of children (113:7–9); to bring the war-mongering counsel of nations to nothing (33:10), and deliver those who fear him from death (33:19). The content of lament has become the reason for praise, though the poet and his community may still be awaiting God's deliverance: "Our soul waits for the LORD; he is our help and shield. *Our heart is glad in him*, because we trust in his holy name" (33:20–21, emphasis mine). Trust enables God's people to move from fear and lament to praise, when God has acted—and when God has yet to set matters right. One other major feature of the Book of Psalms further contributes to this difficult movement from lament to praise.

Learning to Sing Again:
The Book of Psalms

In the early 1970s Gerald Wilson began publishing literature arguing that the Book of Psalms was not an ad hoc collection of individual psalms and groups of psalms but was a carefully crafted and edited collection that presented its own message beyond that of the individual psalms (*The Editing of the Hebrew Psalter*, 1985). Scholars immediately began to put Wilson's hypothesis to the test; forty years and the sacrifice of a small forest of trees later, and the general consensus (with a few holdouts) is that Wilson was right (see J. Clinton McCann, Jr., *Shape and Shaping of the Psalter*, 1993 and Nancy L. deClaisse-Walford, *Reading from the Beginning: The Shaping of the Hebrew Psalter*, 1997). In essence, the Book of Psalms leads its reader through lament to praise.

The Book of Psalms consists of five sub-books: Book One (Pss 1–41), Book Two (42–72), Book Three (73–89), Book Four (90–106), and Book Five (107–150). The short doxologies at the end of Books I-IV denote the end of each book. Psalms 1 and 2, bracketed by a blessing at beginning (1:1) and end (2:11), set out the principle themes of the Book of Psalms: the path of the righteous and the wicked—and their fates—and the antagonism of nations against the LORD's anointed king in Zion.

Immediately, in Book I, the LORD's anointed is under pressure due to enemies (see Pss 3–7). In fact, of the 39 chapters in Book I (excluding chapters 1–2) 18 are laments. Book I ends with a psalm of trust (41) and words that express confidence in the LORD despite all of the threats and troubles that have materialized in Book I:

> By this I know that you are pleased with me;
>> because my enemy has not triumphed over me.
> But you have upheld me because of my integrity,
>> and set me in your presence forever. (Ps 41:11–12)

Book II begins with lament for what appears to be some separation or exile from the presence of God (Ps 42–43); and lament predominates Book II even more than Book I, with 19 laments of the 31 total chapters. The final psalm of Book II prays specifically for the king, that he reign with God's justice for the poor and needy (72:1–4,12–14), and that he live long as a blessing to God's people (72:5–6,15–17) with enemies bowing before him (72:8–11). Book III not only features lament (9 of 17 psalms are laments), but concludes with a psalm that verifies the fall of the nation (Ps 89). The conflict with the nations that began in Psalm 2 has come to a surprise climax. Despite God's promises to the Davidic king (89:19–37), the dynasty has fallen and the nation crushed (89:38–45).

Book IV begins with a lament for the brevity of life—or what might be regarded as a funeral song for the death of the nation (Ps 90). But from this point forward the Book of Psalms turns back toward the LORD with praise—not for a human king or kingdom, but for the LORD's reign over his people. The death of the nation, then, reveals a theological truth, lost through many years and battles to keep the nation alive: the LORD reigns. Psalms 93–99 declare this news with force:

> The LORD is King, he is robed with majesty; (93:1a)

> Rise up, O Judge of the earth;
>> give to the proud what they deserve! (94:2)

> For the LORD is a great God,
>> and a great King above all gods. (95:3)

> Say among the nations, "The LORD is King!
>> The world is firmly established; it shall never
>> be moved.
>> He will judge the peoples with equity." (96:10)

> The LORD is King! Let the earth rejoice;
>> let the many coastlands be glad! (97:1)

> With trumpets and the sound of the horn
>> make a joyful noise before the King, the LORD (98:6)

> The LORD is King; let the peoples tremble!
>> He sits enthroned upon the cherubim, let the earth
>> quake! (99:1)

> Mighty King, lover of justice,
>> you have established equity;
> you have executed justice
>> and righteousness in Jacob. (99:4)

The recognition of the LORD's reign, with its commitment to judgment and justice (e.g., 90:10–13), changes everything for Israel, even if the nation remains subject to Babylon, Persia, Greece, or Rome. Despite appearances, their God reigns.

The final psalm in Book IV confesses Israel's many sins, and prays:

> Save us, O LORD our God,
>> *and gather us from among the nations,*
> that we may give thanks to your holy name
>> and glory in your praise. (Ps 106:47, emphasis mine)

In response, the first psalm of Book Five urges those redeemed by the LORD from various lands to speak of God's deliverance (107:1–3). Books

IV and V lead Israel and the reader back to praise (see Pemberton, *Hurting with God*, 244–245).

The enormous movement from lament (Books I-III) to praise (Books IV-V) in the Book of Psalms matches the movement within laments that urge their readers to praise the LORD: a) now and forever, regardless of circumstances, and b) if God will remove the barricades that obstruct their praise. As the Book of Psalms comes to a close we also discover a trio of new praises awaiting us at the end of the book—praises that know about the Pit and what God does for those who are brokenhearted.

Psalm 145 opens with strong praise for "my God and King" (145:1). The LORD is not only great beyond measure (3) but his works are wondrous and mighty—and demand proclamation from one generation to another (4–13). What the Book of Psalms has taught us by its individual psalms and its structure, this psalmist confirms by a report of God's work in the deep and dark night of the soul:

> The LORD upholds all who are falling,
>> and raises up all who are bowed down. (14)

> The LORD is near to all who call on him,
>> to all who call on him in truth.
> He fulfills the desires of all who fear him;
>> he also hears their cry, and saves them. (18–19)

Psalm 146, a classic hymn of praise, takes up the message in even greater detail. The LORD, whom I will praise as long as I live (146:2), not only made the "heaven and earth, the sea, and all that is in them" (146:6), but he also

> Executes justice for the oppressed (7a)
> Gives food to the hungry (7b)
> Sets prisoners free (7c)
> Opens the eyes of the blind (8a)
> Lifts those bowed down (8b)

> Watches over strangers (9a)
> Upholds the orphan and widow (9b)

So not only has the book taught us that the LORD will reign forever (146:10), but that the LORD is not a God only for the healthy, wealthy, settled, and unbroken. Instead, as the book closes the praise expands to especially notice what God does for those in need.

Psalm 147 sets the exclamation mark to the praise for God's loving concern for the broken. Here, as the LORD rebuilds Jerusalem,

> he gathers the outcasts of Israel.
> He heals the brokenhearted,
>   and binds up their wounds. (2b-3)
>
> The LORD lifts up the downtrodden;
>   he casts the wicked to the ground. (6)

The LORD's delight is not in the strong, fast, or self-reliant (10), but in those who fear him and put their hope in his steadfast love (11).

Conclusions

At first sight it is difficult to imagine how a lament could dare to encourage its reader to praise a God who could fix their problem but has not. The idea seems cold-hearted and cruel. Life may be falling apart, people taking advantage of your weakness, power mongers pushing you out, not to mention how you are losing your family in the process—but hey, don't worry, *Praise the Lord!* I cannot speak for you, but my own response to this idea would never get past the editor. Who would dare to play Bob Marley's, "Don't Worry, Be Happy" in a cancer ward or hospice? And yet if we can hold on for just a little while, the Book of Psalms begins to show us how it is possible to sing praise—even reasonably. As we continue to read we find praises that acknowledge not all is well in God's world. Further along the path, new praises speak of God's work among the broken-hearted and those living in deep darkness. Then finally stepping back to view the book as a whole, we again see lament leading toward praise—because of a God whose preference is not with the strong, self-contained, and well-to-do, but with the weak, the broken, and the poor.

So new songs continue to testify to the LORD's work among the weak (e.g., 33:3, 40:3, 96:1, and 98:1), including a young woman who just had to sing when she learned of the Lord's plan for her life: Mary, the mother-to-be of Jesus. In fact, she found Hannah's song to be the perfect template for her own song, words that have come to be known as the Magnificat.

> My soul magnifies the Lord,
>> and my spirit rejoices in God my Savior,
> for he has looked with favor on the lowliness of
> his servant.
>> Surely, from now on all generations will call
>> me blessed,
> for the Mighty One has done great things for me,
>> and holy is his name.
> His mercy is for those who fear him
>> from generation to generation.
> He has shown strength with his arm;
>> he has scattered the proud in the thoughts of
>> their hearts.
> He has brought down the powerful from their thrones,
>> and lifted up the lowly;
> he has filled the hungry with good things,
>> and sent the rich away empty.
> He has helped his servant Israel,
>> in remembrance of his mercy,
> according to the promise he made to our ancestors
>> to Abraham and to his descendants forever.
> (Lk 1:46–55)

As with Hannah, we need to linger over these words and the one who sings on this day, a young unmarried woman. When the angel came to her to announce what was about to happen, her trust in the Lord was absolute: "Here am I, the servant of the Lord; let it be with me according to your word" (Lk 1:38). Meanwhile her "betrothed," Joseph, required a vision to keep him from quietly divorcing Mary, sparing her (or him?) public disgrace (Matt 1:19–25). I wonder if she had any idea of what it meant to be the mother of this child. After the birth and presentation in the temple, old Simeon would say to Mary: "This child is destined for the falling and the rising of many in Israel, and to be a sign that will be opposed so that the inner thoughts of many will be revealed—*and a sword will pierce your own soul too*" (Lk 2:34–35, emphasis mine). Mary may sing praise, but make no mistake about the sacrifice she too, like Hannah, will make. Praise, old or new, comes with a cost.

CHAPTER SEVEN

Spoke #4:
Rejoicing in the Lord

One evening not long ago our only slightly over-weight Basset Hound, Buford Hercules, burst through his dog door and with all his might began to run in small circles (large circles take too much energy) and bark inside the house—a rare event. He had been outside barking—not a rare event—running up and down the fence line playing with the Dalmatian mom and her nine pups on the other side of the fence. So Buford's sudden, loud, and excited barking inside the house was a clear call that all was not well in his world. Something was terribly wrong. And as soon as I got to a window I could see the problem: somehow one of the Dalmatian pups had managed to get on our side of the fence—into Buford's backyard—and could not get back to her mom. Now it is true that Bassets do not rank highly on breed intelligence scales. Who knows, maybe a poodle would have picked up the pup, set her back where she belonged, and still made her grooming appointment. But Buford was smart enough to know that something did not belong— it was out of place and needed someone to fix the situation—and we were the only ones around to help.

Buford, among others, may have the same reaction to this chapter. Why a chapter about joy and rejoicing when we just spoke about praise in the prior chapter? A number of arguments could be raised for putting the idea of joy back within new praise. For example, 1) the overlap in meaning seems somewhat obvious; to "praise the LORD" carries much the same idea as to "rejoice in the LORD." 2) The two expressions sometimes appear together in the same psalm (e.g., 9:14, 33:1, 75:9). Nonetheless, risking disagreement with a sixty-five pound basset, I find that the concepts of joy and rejoicing warrant full investigation as they raise significant new questions for life after lament

The chapter ahead will begin with an examination of the results of a second survey of laments that lead their readers to joy, a close reading of a psalm of lament that contains a heavy emphasis on joy, and stepping back to view the questions these psalms and the motif of joy raise for life after lament and the reign of God. After these introductory matters set the questions and direction for the chapter we will 1) take note of the many brief references to joy in psalms that come *After Lament* and references to joy in psalms of thanksgiving and psalms of new praise that we have already examined in chapters 5 and 6. 2) Then we will turn to the close reading of five psalms of joy, keeping in mind the questions raised above (in the introduction). 3) Finally, I will provide an analysis of the issues at stake in the psalms that carry a motif of joy.

Introducing Joy

1. The Lament Psalms

In chapter 3 I stated that a small group of lament psalms primarily urge their readers to rejoice. These psalms fell into two categories: 1) texts with promises that the poet and others will rejoice in the LORD *if* the LORD will deliver them or answer their prayer (e.g., 58, 64), and 2) texts that assure God that they will rejoice in the LORD no matter what may happen (e.g., 31, 70).

A second layer to this survey considers the relationship of the enemy to the theme of joy. As in the laments in general, nearly all the psalms that include some idea of joy include the problem of an enemy, usually a human threat. On the one hand, some writers beg the LORD not to let the enemy rejoice over them. For example, if the LORD fails to provide what is needed, the poet writes, "my enemy will say, 'I have prevailed'; my foes will rejoice because I am shaken" (13:4). Or as another psalmist prays, "Only do not let them rejoice over me, those who boast against me when my foot slips" (38:16, see also 71:23). On the other hand, most lament psalms with the motif of joy ask the LORD to save the poet and her community so they can rejoice. For example, the poet in Psalm 9 asks the LORD to see what he is suffering so that the LORD will put an end to it "so that I may recount your praises, and . . . rejoice in your deliverance" (9:13–14). Or, the writer of Psalm 42–43 begs the LORD to vindicate him against ungodly enemies (43:1) and asks, "Why must I walk about mournfully because of the oppression of the enemy?" (43:2). But when God brings the psalmist home, defeating all opposition, the poet writes, "I will go to the altar of God, to *God my exceeding joy*; and I will praise you with the harp, O God, my God" (43:4, emphasis mine). So then, the writers' concern is for enemies who will rejoice over them, unless God acts so that the psalmists and their communities may rejoice in victory over the enemy (13:5, 35:9) or rejoice in God's vengeance against the enemy (58:10, 137:8–9). As an aside, sometimes the enemy is not a human, but the human problem of sin and need for forgiveness that will bring joy. So we read in Psalm 51: Let me hear joy and gladness; let the bones that you have crushed rejoice... Restore to me the joy of your salvation, and sustain in me a willing spirit. (51:8,12, see also 85:6, 90:14)

2. Psalm 35

Of the laments **Psalm 35** carries an unusually high density of words for happiness: joy, rejoice, exult, glee, be glad. A close reading of this psalm will help us understand how this cluster of ideas works in the Psalms. Psalm 35 unfolds in three distinct movements (vv. 1–10, 11–18, 19–28).

Movement I: In verses 1–3 a barrage of military images assaults the enemy as the writer asks God to contend, fight, "take hold of shield and buckler," and "draw the spear and javelin." A bombardment of wishes against the enemy continues in verses 3–8:

> Let them be put to shame and dishonor
> Let them be turned back and confounded
> Let them be like chaff before the wind
>   (with an angel driving them on)
> Let their way be dark and slippery
>   (with an angel pursuing them)
> Let ruin come on them unawares
> Let the net they hid ensnare them
> Let them fall in it—to their ruin

Within these lines we also begin to get a glimpse of what has happened and why God should deploy an all-out offensive. According to the poet, these enemies "seek after my life" (4a), "devise evil against me" (4b), and for no fault of my own they lay hidden nets and pits (7).

Movement II: The second movement of Psalm 35 takes us to court in the city gate where malicious witnesses testify against the writer and ask incriminating questions he cannot answer (11). As the psalmist recalls his past interaction with those now making accusations, he remembers when they were sick and in need. The writer did all he knew to do to appeal for God's healing: he wore sackcloth, fasted, prayed with bowed head, grieved, mourned, and lamented intensely for them as if they were his mother. But now at his stumbling these same people gather "in glee" against him, bringing in even more people to testify with false charges (15–16). The very people he prayed for have turned into roaring lions that tear into his flesh (17).

Movement III: The final movement is filled with the psalmist's requests of God: a) Do not let my "treacherous enemies *rejoice* over me" or those who hate me for no reason succeed in their plans (19, emphasis mine). These are the people who speak deceitful words against the innocent (20) and open their mouths against me with false testimony, saying, "our eyes have seen it" (21). b) You, God, are the one who has seen everything; do not withhold your testimony (22). Wake up! Get up for my defense (23) and vindicate me: "do not let them *rejoice* over me" and do not let them get what they want (24, emphasis mine). c) "Let all those who *rejoice* at my calamity" be shamed, confused, and dishonored (26, emphasis mine). d) Let those who want my vindication "*shout for joy* and *be glad*" (27, emphasis mine), and be able to say: "Great is the LORD, who delights in the welfare of his servant" (27).

Finally, each movement concludes with a statement of what the writer will do in response to God's help. I. Then "my soul shall *rejoice in the Lord, exulting* in his deliverance," because the LORD delivers the weak from the strong (9–10, emphasis mine). II. Then "I will thank you in the great congregation" (18). III. "Then my tongue shall tell of your righteousness (victory) and of your praise all day long" (28).

3. Conclusions and Questions

At stake in Psalm 35 is who will win the power struggle and rejoice: 1) the strong, deceptive, cunning, malicious, two-faced liars who have no regard for those who care for them, or 2) the writer and his community who have been duped by the lies and deception, and who invested themselves in the well-being of others only to be turned on and attacked like a lion. The question is not merely which side God will support, but what kind of God will the LORD be and who will be the ones to rejoice under the LORD's rule? Will it be the power-monger who makes his way to the top by deception, stepping on others who are quickly dismissed lest they talk? Will it be those who fool everyone until the moment of truth arrives and suddenly everything changes? Malicious witnesses are in place, false accusations fly like arrows, and the one for whom I spent myself returns my efforts with a dagger in my back. Or will the LORD show himself to be a warrior on behalf of the weak, a lion tamer for those under threat, and an attorney for the exposed? Who does the LORD want to rejoice in his kingdom? The LORD must decide and act, because inaction is *de facto* support of the powerful.

The same kingdom values are at stake in the psalms of lament that beg the LORD for the poets to rejoice instead of their opponents: who will find joy in the kingdom of God? Will those who trust in God's steadfast love be able to rejoice in God's salvation or will my enemies prevail and rejoice because I am shaken? (13:4–5, also 38:15–16, 89:42) Will God pay attention to those who trust him and are suffering due to their enemies, and deliver them? (9:13–14) Will God watch the back of his people who take refuge in him, vindicating them against an ungodly people? (43:1–4, 71:20–24) Will God forgive those who turn to him and turn away from anger? (51:8, 12, 85:1–6, 90:13–14)

Who rejoices in the kingdom of God is a crucial policy decision for the reign of God. The laments that encourage the reader to rejoice also challenge the LORD to keep promises made on the campaign trail. Will those seek refuge in the LORD (2:12, 5:11, 20:4), those guilty of sin and in need of forgiveness (51:8,12, 85:6, 90:14), and the weak that suffer at the hands of their enemies (9:14, 13:4–5, 43:1–5, 71:22–24)—will these be the ones who rejoice under God's reign? Or will it be the strong that speak warmly about God in public, but in private deny the LORD by their actions? Will it be those who deceptively worm their way into positions of power, or those who take advantage of God's people? Will these be the ones who find joy? These laments ask just what kind of place this is going to be? What will the reign of God establish? Will it be any different from other nations or people with their gods who jockey for power and position? Or will it be business as usual? The LORD will decide by who laughs and who does not.

The Kingdom of Rejoicing

The Psalms of Joy

Many psalms that come *After Lament* include fleeting references to joy. A few of these testimonies occur at the beginning of the psalm:

> O come, let us sing to the LORD;
>> let us *make a joyful noise* to the rock of our salvation!

> Let us come into his presence with thanksgiving;
>> let us *make a joyful noise* to him with songs of praise!
>> (95:1–2, emphasis mine; see also 105:3)

More often these statements appear at the conclusion of the psalm:

> Therefore *my heart is glad*, and *my soul rejoices*;
>> my body also rests secure.
> For you do not give me up to Sheol,
>> or let your faithful one see the Pit.
> You show me the path of life.
>> In your presence there is *fullness of joy*;
>> in your right hand are *pleasures forevermore* (16:9–11,
>> emphasis mine)

> Let the nations *be glad and sing for joy*,
>> for you judge the peoples with equity
>> and guide the nations upon the earth. *Selah*
> Let the peoples praise you, O God;
>> let all the peoples praise you. (67:4–5, emphasis mine
>> see also 40:16)

And naturally, some acclamations of joy come in the middle of the psalm:

> This is the day that the LORD has made;
> *let us rejoice* and *be glad in it*. (118:24; emphasis mine
> see also 149:2–5)

Passing references to joy also appear in hymns that celebrate the king's victory (21:6), the king's wedding (45:7–8, 15), and the procession of the Ark to its resting place (132:9, 16).

Notable in these citations is the close proximity of affirmations that the LORD is king. Psalm 95:1–3: let us make a joyful noise, *because the Lord is a great king*. Psalm 67:4: let the nations sing for joy because *the Lord judges* the peoples with equity *and guides nations*—both royal tasks. And although Psalm 118 lacks the explicit terminology, it certainly affirms the LORD to be king (see esp. vv. 8–9, 15–16, 21–23, 27). For these brief acclamations of joy or rejoicing, the larger context celebrates the LORD as king.

We have also examined a number of psalms in prior chapters in which the motif of joy appears. Most notably, Psalm 30 (chapter 5) told us that "Weeping may linger for the night, but joy comes with the morning" (30:5b), and even more:

> You have turned my mourning into dancing;
>> you have taken off my sackcloth
>> and clothed me with joy,
> so that my soul may praise you and not be silent.
> O LORD my God, I will give thanks to you forever.
> (30:11–12)

While Psalm 30 may lack royal ideology, Psalm 33 (chapter 6) leaves little doubt, beginning with an appeal: "Rejoice in the LORD, O you righteous. Praise befits the upright" (33:1), then later explaining, "Happy is the nation who God is the LORD, the people whom he has chosen as his heritage" (33:12). The happiness or joy of the nation is directly related to its ownership, its divine king. In Psalm 66 (chapter 5) the opening line says, "Make a joyful noise to God, all the earth," and leads to ideas that support the motif that the LORD is king, such as how all the earth worships and cringes before God's great power (66:1–3). Like Psalm 66, Psalm 92 (chapter 5) says, "For you, O LORD, have made me glad by your work; at the works of your hands I sing for joy" (92:4), while including royal ideas such as God's enemies will perish and be scattered (92:9).

Though the evidence in these brief statements of joy may be inconclusive, what does appear supports earlier claims in this chapter: who rejoices in the Kingdom of God is an indicator of the highest values and commitments of the king. This principle is further confirmed by close reading of five psalms that have special emphasis on joy or rejoicing.

Five Psalms of Joy

Psalm 65 originates as part of the fulfillment of a vow (65:1), most likely made during a time of crisis. The final verses of the psalm celebrate ample rains and an abundant harvest (9–13); consequently, the disaster prompting the vow was most likely a famine due to drought. We may also safely surmise that the psalmist's community has interpreted the drought as a punishment for their sin (2–3), which God has forgiven, as the rains now demonstrate. The psalm, then, is a celebration for both forgiveness of sin and the rains that have replenished pasture land, meadows, and valleys for grazing flocks and herds (12–13), and generously watered cultivated fields to provide food for people (9–11).

The psalmist is quick to set the LORD's answer to his people's needs within a "global" context (5–8). The LORD is not for Israel alone, but is "the hope of all the ends of the earth" (5). God not only established the mountains by his might or strength, but is the one who silences "the roaring of the seas." This reference could indicate limiting the seas at creation, or by means of synonymous parallelism to the next line, the roaring seas may denote the uproar or tumult of "the peoples" (i.e., nations). Thus, the psalmist, overwhelmed by the needed rains, extends praise to include God's creation; or more likely, here we find a final piece of the background story: with the LORD's help a recent national threat has also been calmed or resolved.

As a consequence of God's work, explicit references to happiness and joy fill the psalm. To begin, the poet states that "Praise is due" to God (1). The people God has chosen are "happy" and satisfied with the goodness that comes from living in God's presence (4). But those who live at "earth's farthest bounds" are also awed by the LORD's work, and the places where morning and evening originate ("the gateways of the morning and the evening") "shout for joy" (8). Closer to home, God the cosmic farmer has been at work; everywhere his wagon or chariot has gone has produced overwhelming fertility (11). (See Clifford, *Psalms 1–72* and Murphy, *Gift of the Psalms*, 106). The "pastures of the wilderness" overflow with growth, while the hills "gird themselves with joy"

(12); the image pictures the hills with such lavish growth that a joyous belt must be brought to hold back the bursting fertility. The meadows, newly clothed with grazing flocks, and valleys decked out with grain also join the celebration as "they shout and sing together for joy" (13).

Without doubt the people who have endured the drought and famine also rejoice when the rains return and grasses begin to grow (for other possible origins see Clifford, *Psalms 1–72*, 302, and Gorgen, *Psalms,* 121). "Happy" (NRSV) or "Blessed" (TNIV) are those chosen by God to live in his presence (4). But in this psalm the only ones rejoicing—shouting for joy (8), girding themselves with joy (12), and singing together for joy (13) are members of nature: the gateways of morning and evening (8), the pastures and hills (12), and the meadows and valleys (13). Indeed, as Novice Maria sings in the *Sound of Music,* "The hills are alive with the sound of music."

Psalm 96 is the first of a trio of psalms consumed by joy (Pss 96–98, see also 95:1–2). This "new song" (96:1) offers two elaborate calls to praise (1–6, 7–13). The first summons ("sing"—repeated 3 times) calls upon all the earth to sing to the LORD and bless his name (1-2a), before turning to Israel and calling her to tell of God's salvation every day and declare his glory and marvelous work among all nations (2b-3). In support of the summons, the poet exclaims that the LORD is a great God, far above all other gods because they are no more than worthless idols (4). In contrast, the LORD is the one who made the heavens (5) and who is the true king escorted by honor and majesty, while strength and beauty remain in his throne room ("sanctuary," 6).

The second summons expands the global vision of the psalm as it calls all the earth to praise God ("ascribe to the LORD" repeated 3 times, 7-8a) and to bring an offering into the LORD's courts (8). Either the nations or Israel is also directed to declare among the nations: "The LORD is king!" (10a). As a result of the LORD's reign, the poet explains a) the earth is firmly established, and b) the LORD will judge all nations with equity or fairness (10).

The declaration of the LORD's reign and his coming to set things right on earth sets off a fireworks display of joy in the heavens and on earth:

> Let the heavens be glad
> Let the earth rejoice
> Let the sea roar
>> (and all that fills it)
> Let the field exult
>> (and everything in it) (edited from 11-12a)

Then in the grand finale: "all the trees of the forest sing for joy" (12b). Similar to Psalm 65 nature alone rejoices and takes up the song of joy; though here the spectacular praise is because the LORD, now enthroned, "is coming to judge the earth" (13). He will set matters right in the world, according to fair standards of rightness and truth (13).

It is remarkable that in our first two psalms of joy, those rejoicing are elements of nature—not humanity or even Israel. When Israel sins and God inflicts a drought (Ps 65; see also 1 Kgs 17:1), God's people suffer, but secondary to the hardship inflicted on nature. So when the rains return it is little wonder that in a poet's imagination the natural world is the first and loudest to rejoice and sing for joy (65:12–13). Perhaps in the same way, when we push the LORD away as king, the first to suffer and those that suffer the most are the innocent: the sea (and all that fills it), the fields (and everything in them), and the trees of the forest. These writers cannot make the sharp division between nature and humanity that we assume every day. For them, the innocents devastated by our sin are water, fields, and trees—and this is long before the industrialization and deforestation of the modern era. In ways we can see and ways we cannot, we have a poor track record as God's representatives charged with caring for creation (Ps 8:4–8, Gen 1:26–28). So when God retakes the throne and declares a campaign on earth to set things as they ought to be, all nature bursts into celebration.

With minimal difference, Psalm 96 also appears in 1 Chronicles 16:23–33 as one of the psalms sung after David brought the Ark of the Covenant (God's throne, see Lev. 16:2 and Ps 99:1) into a tent in Jerusalem (1 Chron 15:1–16:6). The occasion represented a renewal of the covenant (1 Chron 16:7–22) and a renewal of the monarchy—the reign of the LORD, not David's dynasty. Consequently, scholars typically regard Psalm 96 as an enthronement psalm that celebrates the renewed reign of God. Some further suggest that this psalm may have been part of an annual festival that replayed the common ancient Near Eastern myth of the battle of the gods with the victor crowned as king and celebrated as the Creator of the universe.

Psalm 97 continues the theme of the LORD's reign (Pss 93–99) announcing that "the LORD is king" (NRSV) or perhaps "the LORD has become king," also recognizing that the ancient Near Eastern battle myth may stand behind this psalm. The announcement of the LORD's great victory and enthronement brings joy and gladness to the earth, both near ("the earth") and far away ("the coastlands" (97:1). The proclamation of the LORD's reign is followed by a second proclamation: the LORD is coming to make an appearance on earth (in literary terms a "theophany"). In order to describe the indescribable, the poet engages his imagination and draws from stock images used in the ancient world to portray the victorious divine warrior—usually the storm god Baal. The grand reversal here, of course, is that images typically used to describe Baal's victory have been co-opted by the poet and reversed to proclaim the LORD is king, not Baal.

The LORD comes wrapped in clouds for royal robes, sitting on a throne with a foundation set in righteousness and justice (2)—not raw power or political maneuvering. Ahead of the LORD a detachment of fire moves about, torching every enemy and every threat to the LORD's good reign (3). As the king gets closer to the earth, a lightning show erupts that illuminates the night sky and thunders with such power that the earth trembles (4). The mountains can cope with the thunder and lightning, but as the LORD gets closer they melt like cheap candles (5). Meanwhile the heavens that have elsewhere proclaimed God's glory (19:1) and grandeur (8:3) now speak of the LORD's righteousness (96:6).

Finally, people begin to get a glimpse of the king's glory (6b) with one of two predictable reactions: 1) those who worship other gods are shamed as their gods bow before the LORD; they recognize their gods are nothing more than useless idols (7), or 2) the king's people are glad and rejoice, not because of the power on display, but because of the character of their God. The LORD is high above the earth, including every other god (9), and his judgments are reliable—loving and guarding the lives of his faithful against the conspiracies of the wicked (10). The king's presence represents the dawn of a new day for the righteous, a time of joy rather than sorrow (11). And so the psalm concludes:

> Rejoice in the LORD, O you his righteous,
> and give thanks to his holy name! (97:12)

For the LORD's people joy comes from the character of the LORD's reign: the magnitude of his strength is matched only by the magnitude of his commitment to fairness and equity, and his fidelity to those who are faithful to him.

Psalm 98 makes explicit what Psalm 96 and 97 have implied: the LORD has won a great victory.

> His right hand and his holy arm
> have gotten him victory. (98:1)

> The LORD has made known his victory. (2)

> All the ends of the earth have seen
> the victory of our God. (3)

Equally important, at least for the LORD's people, is that while the LORD has won a great victory that proves he is king, the LORD still "remembers" or keeps his love and commitment to small, insignificant Israel (3). Little wonder the poet calls for a new song (1), and for all the earth to make a *joyful* noise, breaking out into a *joyous* song (4). Bring all the musical instruments together—lyre, trumpets, whatever you can find, and "make a *joyful noise* before the King, the LORD" (6, emphasis mine).

Extend a joyous welcome to the king who is coming to reign over an upside-down kingdom; where a great universal king has chosen the small house of Israel.

The poet's imagination takes flight (much as in 96:10–13). Let the chaotic sea, brought under control at creation, but ever threatening to break out—let this sea join the joyful noise with its roar; and while we are at it, let's get the world and all who live in it to sing along (7). This poet would not only like to teach the world to sing, she is doing it. The floodwaters can clap their hands, holding down the rhythm; and the hills have had enough practice now to sing along in perfect harmony— all for joy (8)—and all because the LORD has become king. And the king is coming to judge the world now, not just at the end of time—an idea that does not send God's people into irrational fear, but singing a new song of joy. The king is coming to set things right, not on the basis of power and money, but on the basis of right-ness and equity.

⌇

I recognize that one could make an argument for including all of the enthronement psalms from this section of Psalms (93–99) in this discussion of joy. My narrow selection is based simply on the intensity of the motif of joy or happiness; and to me, Psalms 96–98 leapt off the page with joy. I also recognize that these psalms might be considered part of one's world before lament, part of the psalms of orientation (as I did in *Hurting with God*, 244). Nonetheless, the remarkable presence of joy in these psalms is the result of a struggle and victory.

I want to make two observations about Psalms 96–98 before moving to the final psalm of joy. First, Psalms 96 and 98 both begin with the same phrase: "O sing to the LORD a new song." A few interpreters argue that this phrase is just another way of stating the call to worship, but with Limburg and Mays I am not ready to dismiss the phrase so quickly. Limburg interacts with this unique call by writing:

Here is a call to break out of traditional ruts and bring some fresh music into the worship service! Since this call also occurs elsewhere (see Ps. 96:1; also 33:3; 40:3; 144:9; 149:1; Isa. 42:10), the point appears to have been an important one to make. There must have been those who wanted only the "old songs" (the good old hymns that everybody knows) and those who wanted to make use of some contemporary ones. This psalm (and the ones listed above) is on the side of those who want to try something new. (*Psalms,* 331)

Limburg's contemporary reading of the situation may not be precisely what the poet was arguing for, however, as Limburg states later: "If God does some new things, then there ought to be some new songs of praise celebrating them" (*Psalms, 331).* As long as God is still at work in our world doing new things, we must continue to write new hymns of praise.

Second, some difference of opinion surrounds the phrase "he is coming to judge the earth" (Ps 96:13 and 98:9). Do these psalms look toward an event at the end of time or are they thinking of one of the LORD's many engagements with his world? Like most psalms, the language is ambiguous enough that it may be read either way; and I suppose either reading is appropriate as long as we do not read the LORD off his throne and away from on-going interaction (including judgment) with the world he rules.

One reading of these psalms (96–98) has become both a reading practiced each Christmas (Revised Common Lectionary) and a new song that proclaims the LORD, our king who has indeed come. The first two verses read:

> Joy to the world!
> The LORD is come: let earth receive her King.
> Let every heart prepare him room, and heaven and
> nature sing.

Joy to the world!

The Savior reigns: let all their songs employ,

while fields and floods, rocks, hills, and plains repeat the
sounding joy.

—Isaac Watts, 1719

Isaac Watts could not have captured the ideas of Psalms 96–98 any better than he did in "Joy to the World," though I wonder if we notice the words we sing. The joy that has come to the world is the reign of her (our) king, a reign of truth and grace (verse 4). So let every heart prepare room for this king, while all heaven and nature sings (verse 1)—even more, "while fields and flocks, rocks, hills, and plains repeat the sounding joy" (verse 2). Joy in the reign of the LORD is human but also in nature, because the LORD has come with a reign of truth and grace to set things right.

❧

Psalm 126 asks us to remember the last time something caused us to laugh so hard that tears trickled down our face, creating their own small river, and we couldn't catch our breath. We fell to the floor, still laughing, clutching our arms across our belly trying to stop laughing, but also in hopes that we didn't pull a muscle; but we couldn't stop. Laughter. Do you remember? *That's what it was like.*

Or do you recall the last time something so wonderful happened that you asked a friend to pinch you, just so you knew this (whatever it may be) was not a dream. So they pinched and you had a small bruise for two weeks. It was not a dream. But it still felt like a dream, too good to be true—something that happens to other people, but not you. A Dream. Do you remember? *That's what it was like.*

That's what it was like when the LORD restored the fortunes of Zion, when the LORD brought back those who had been exiled so far away (126:1). Oh, that was a good day. It was like a dream (1b) and we couldn't stop laughing or shouting for pure joy (2a). The word spread among the nations, "The LORD has done great things for them" (2b). But back home we couldn't escape seeing and experiencing what the LORD had done for us; and there was no way we could stop rejoicing in our God.

But the pessimists are right, those brilliant analysts on the sideline of life who tell us not to get so carried away because it's not going to last. They are correct; no great moment lasts forever—not a championship, a wedding, a fiftieth anniversary, or a graduation. But instead of dropping our heads in defeat and letting moments of joy float away, that's when we must catch them, hold them as long as we can—maybe even breath in some of the helium and speak with funny voices until the moment is over. Yes, it is safer and much more predictable to stand on the sidelines and warn other people about the temporal nature of joy, how it is not going to last. But life is living in the moment. As the writer of Ecclesiastes put it: "There is nothing better for mortals than to eat and drink, and find enjoyment in their toil. This also, I saw, is from the hand of God; for apart from him who can eat or who can have enjoyment?" (Eccles. 2:24–25).

Back in Jerusalem, however, the pessimists are gloating; the pendulum has swung and joy has been suspended until the LORD intervenes (4). True to her tribe, the psalmist provides no details about what has happened. We know from other sources that life in Jerusalem after the exile was not exactly all that the travel brochure promised (see Isa 40–55). The former proud nation of Judah is now nothing more than a small province in the Persian empire. Zion/Jerusalem, with all her psalms of beauty, strength, and stability (Pss 46, 48, 84, 122), has been replaced by Mizpah as the administrative capital. And economic conditions are deplorable; debt slavery is on the rise, even the sale of children. So it may be that nothing happened between verses 3 and 4 except that those who returned with such joy have now fully recognized the realities of life back home in Jerusalem. Their newfound awareness does not take away the joy of coming back home (1–3), but it does turn them toward the LORD who printed the travel brochure. They recognize a need for the most fundamental necessity of life: water. They need the rain of which Psalm 65 spoke (65:9–13). The restoration of their fortunes begins (or ends) with rain that will fill the dry stream beds in the Southern land (Negeb, 4): rain that will transform those who carry seed to the field weeping, and those sowing the seed through tears. Everything rides on this planting—sowing seed they cannot afford to plant. What are they to eat? Only rain can transform them into reapers who return home with the harvest, shouting for joy! The gamble, however, is enormous—risking their lives with this one planting in hope that the king will turn their tears of desperation into tears of joy.

Conclusions

I

I hope that as you come out of a season of lament you find the language of joy to be the best, most appropriate language for your situation. And if this is your story I urge you not to hold back or listen to the pessimists. Rejoice in the LORD! Sing with joy! Stand in the rain and let joy saturate even your best raincoat (Ps 65). Recognize the king who has answered your prayers, restoring your life by giving what you asked for or what you never dreamed might happen (Ps 126).

II

Some of the laments urged us to rejoice in the LORD and assured God that we will rejoice no matter what may happen (e.g., 31, 70). Psalms 96–98 explain how such rejoicing is possible, even when our lives are in turmoil and our prayers seem to be falling on deaf ears. 1) The LORD reigns or has become king (96:10, 97:1, 98:6). And as king, 2) the LORD is coming to set things right ("to judge," 96:10, 13, 97:2–12, 98:9). Consequently, we may rejoice in the LORD as an act of praise because the king deserves our joyful praise; and we can rejoice because we know that sooner (we hope) or later God will intervene in human affairs to set matters as they ought to be. The LORD's reign is a kingdom of joy.

III

Getting what we want or most need is not the only path to joy in the kingdom of God. In the summer of 2010 my life was defined by pain, the pain of a divorce after twenty-six years of marriage and the physical pain in my left lower leg and foot, and by summer's end the same pain in my right lower leg and foot. I was devastated by a lack of hope.

I'm no super-saint, but I knew that the only place I might find enough hope to get through the next week was church—I needed it worse than a junkie needs a fix. But getting to church (and staying) was becoming more and more difficult. The first Sunday in September I slept through my alarm, missed Bible classes, and then got up with hard pain in both legs. I was late, so the only parking was in outer lots, a long painful walk to the auditorium. A woman who knew about pain presided over the Holy Communion. She spoke about her divorce, the pain in her life, and the challenges we all face. Then she asked us to turn to the person sitting next to us and say, "God gets it." I tried, but I couldn't get the words out of my mouth. Tears came instead, weeping I could not control. God understands my life? God gets my pain and hopelessness?

That day marked a turning point for me (and others) as the woman's words became the catalyst for a small group of believers in deep pain to begin meeting together, sharing our stories. A small group saved my life in the fall of 2010. And without either of us looking or even thinking about it, I began to fall in love with the woman who spoke that Sunday, and she with me. A year later, July 9, I married Dana (Hood)—and I was totally surprised by joy. God did not take away my pain, or even make it a little better. I did not get what I hoped for. But today if God were to insult me with an offer, You may keep Dana or lose the pain, I would choose Dana; with her I can live with the pain. Sometimes in the midst of our pain God surprises us with joy we never expected.

CHAPTER EIGHT

Spoke #5: Psalms of Instruction

Because of my years devoted to teaching ministries in churches and universities, it pains me to admit that theology (what we believe to be true about God, the world, and our life with God) is best taught and reinforced through song, not sermon or lecture. In classroom and sanctuary, learning is a passive affair: the transmission of information from an active teacher or preacher to a passive audience. Sometimes the teacher/preacher has a gift for communicating in such a setting, and others use methods that engage the audience in more active learning. Nonetheless, we are no match for a song that an audience not only hears, but sings. In the case of a popular hymn, we may sing the hymn every other week or at least once or twice a month for a year, repeating and impressing the theological ideas deep on the hearts of worshippers. A preacher's sermon doesn't stand a chance against the words of a hymn.

If You Can't Beat 'em, Join 'em

While every psalm teaches theology in some way, a few psalms explicitly take instruction to be their primary goal—a point to which we will return momentarily. First, we need to consider the inter-play between lament and instruction that we introduced in chapter 3. Not many laments direct their readers toward seeking instruction from the LORD. Only ten percent or so of the laments ask the LORD to teach them (25:4, 27:11, 51:6, 86:11, 90:12, 143:8, 10). Notably, with the exception of Psalms 27 and 143, each of these requests is set in psalms that seek forgiveness:

Psalm 25— teach [*lmd*] me your paths. (4b)

> Do not remember the sins of my youth or
> my transgression;
>> according to your steadfast love remember me,
>> for your goodness' sake, O LORD! (7)

> For your name's sake, O LORD,
>> pardon my guilt, for it is great. (11)

> Consider my affliction and my trouble,
>> and forgive all my sins. (18)

Psalm 51— teach [*yd'*] me wisdom in my secret heart. (6b)

> Have mercy on me, O God,
>> according to your steadfast love;
> according to you abundant mercy
>> blot out my transgressions.
> Wash me thoroughly from my iniquity,
>> and cleanse me from my sin. (1–2)

Psalm 86— Teach [*yrh*] me your way, O LORD,
>> that I may walk in your truth;
>> give me an undivided heart to revere your name. (11)

> Gladden the soul of your servant,
>> for to you, O LORD, I lift up my soul.
> For you, O LORD, are good and forgiving,
>> abounding in steadfast love to all who call on you.
>> (4–5)

Psalm 90— So teach [*yd'*] us to count our days
　　　　that we may gain a wise heart. (12)

　　You have set our iniquities before you,
　　　　our secret sins in the light of your countenance . . .
　　Turn, O LORD! How long?
　　　　Have compassion on your servants! (8,13)

We may tentatively conclude that these psalmists regard forgiveness as incomplete without divine instruction that will help them know the way in which they should go, or the path they should take. Thus, their requests for mercy include appeals for direction.

　　The exceptions, Psalms 27 and 143, both seek the LORD's instruction in view of a threat from enemies.

Psalm 27— Teach [*yrh*] me your way, O LORD,
　　　　and lead me on a level path
　　　　because of my enemies. (27:11)

Psalm 143— Let me hear of your steadfast love in the morning,
　　　　for in you I put my trust.
　　Teach [*lmd*] me the way I should go,
　　　　for to you I lift up my soul.
　　Save me, O LORD, from my enemies;
　　　　I have fled to you for refuge. (143:8–9)

The same alarm for enemies is present in two of the psalms above that are concerned for forgiveness.

Psalm 25— O my God, in you I trust;
　　　　do not let me be put to shame;
　　　　do not let my enemies exult over me. (25:2)

　　teach [*lmd*] me your paths. (25:4b)

　　He leads the humble in what is right,
　　　　and teaches [*lmd*] the humble his way. (25:9)

Psalm 86— Teach [*yrh*] me your way, O LORD,
　　　　that I may walk in your truth;
　　　　give me an undivided heart to revere your name. (11)

　　O God, the insolent rise up against me;
　　　　a band of ruffians seeks my life,
　　　　and they do not set you before them. (86:14)

In these cases, the poets regard the LORD's instruction as critical for escaping the danger of the enemy. Consequently, the laments that call for God's instruction do so out of an immediate threat, whether the danger of sin or enemies, or both.

Various Hebrew terms for teaching occur far more frequently in Psalm 119, a massive acrostic created by sages (and so designated a Wisdom psalm). Following the work of Will Soll (*Psalm 119: Matrix, Form, and Setting*, 1991), however, Psalm 119 also appears to be a lament with all the typical elements of the genre repeated over and over again, what I would have to admit to be a major oversight in my prior work on lament—an oversight on the order of cataloging the most important ship wrecks of all time and failing to mention the Titanic. The request for God's instruction or direction recurs frequently in this psalm: teach me (*lmd*, 12, 26, 64, 66, 68, 108, 124, 135, 171), give me understanding (*byn*, 27, 34, 73, 104, 125, 144, 169), teach me (*yrh*, 33, 102), teach me (*khwn*, 29).

However, what the psalmists want to learn from God or God's instruction is at best vague. Outside Psalm 119 the requests ask to learn about "your paths" (25:4), "your way" (27:11, 86:11), "your will" (143:10), "the way I should go" (143:8), "wisdom" (51:6), or most specifically, "to count our days" (90:12). Within Psalm 119 the sages ask God to "teach me" (*lmd*): "your statutes" (12, 26, 64, 68, 124, 135, 171), "your ordinances" (108), and "good judgment and knowledge" (66). Or to teach (*yrh*) me "the way of your statutes" (33) or "graciously teach (*khwn*) me your law" (29). In one case the writer declares that "through your precepts I get understanding" (104). Elsewhere they ask God to "give me understanding" (*byn*):

- according to your word (169)
- that I might keep your law (34)
- that I might learn your commandments (73)
- that I may know your decrees (125)
- that I may live (144)

And yet despite an initial appearance of clarity in Psalm 119, the content of what the writer hopes to learn from God's instruction is left unspecified and vague. Like Superman in Macy's Thanksgiving Day Parade, we know there is something inside because if we let go of the ropes Superman will indeed fly, but the magic elixir is hidden beyond our sight.

I remember a time not so long ago when churches sang many more songs of instruction and encouragement for right living than we do today. Songs such as "Angry Words," "How Shall the Young Secure Their Hearts?" and "Are You Sowing the Seed of the Kingdom, Brother?" which I recall better as "Are You Sowing the Seed of the King, Dumb Brother?"—which suggests we youngsters were not securing our hearts all that well. Then a number of good-hearted people began to be concerned that we were not praising God with our songs about the church and right living, a point that merits serious consideration. It is easy to misplace the emphasis of our worship on something or someone other than God. So the pendulum began to swing toward worship and praise songs that infrequently provide instruction or encouragement in Christian living. Some have even gone to the extreme of reckoning such songs illegitimate because they do not worship God. So, if nothing else, the recognition here that the laments direct us toward instruction and teaching psalms which are part of the Book of Psalms should help us see that many types of songs praise God—including those in which we teach and encourage one another in right living.

This much is certain. Some laments direct their readers toward much-needed instruction in God's way. We may look for and find suitable instruction for these psalms in the sage's books of Proverbs and Ecclesiastes, or beyond the sages in the Torah (Law) or Prophets. However, the instruction to which the laments refer may also be found within the Book of Psalms. Research consistently identifies eight psalms as Wisdom or Torah Psalms: 1, 37, 49, 73, 112, 119, 127, and 128. These are psalms whose primary purpose is to teach the reader or convey a lesson. In addition, various interpreters suggest six other psalms that might also be Wisdom or Torah Psalms: 14, 19:7–14, 32, 36, 78, and 133. In this chapter we will read four of these psalms, two from each list, in order to illustrate the type of instruction to which the laments point their readers within the Book of Psalms.

Four Psalms of Instruction

Psalm 127 is one of the "Psalms of Ascent" (120–134), possibly a pilgrimage song for those traveling to worship at the Jerusalem temple. The text consists of two halves (1–2 and 3–5) that appear to have little in common; so little, in fact, that we might wonder if these verses belong together or if two short psalm fragments have been indiscriminately put together so that we do not accidently lose one or the other.

Part I: Verses one and two feature the word "in vain," perhaps best understood as "ineffective" or "unsuccessful" in three scenarios: building a house, guarding a city, and anxious work from sun-up until sundown.

The first scenario plays with the image of house building and the futility of building a house without the LORD's blessing or participation; the house is destined to collapse. Without denying this picture of an actual house with men wasting their hard work and sweat on a doomed project, this image may be the vehicle of additional ideas. For example, house building might denote a husband and wife building their home or family with all the details surrounding such an enterprise. Unless the LORD is at the heart of their marriage and they rely on the LORD's guidance and blessing instead of their own ingenuity, their efforts will be unsuccessful. (I grew up with a regular dosage of this understanding of the psalm applied at least once a year from middle school until high school graduation.)

Or maybe the message at hand speaks to the royal dynasty ("house") of David. The LORD promised to build David a "house" (dynasty) when David was planning to build the LORD's "house" (temple; 2 Sam 7:11–12); despite all the threats and disruption in the house of David, the psalm reminds everyone, not the least all the royal advisors, that the single most important factor in David's regime is the LORD's support.

Or considering Psalm 127 as a pilgrimage song ("Psalm of Ascents"), perhaps the house is The House, God's dwelling place in Jerusalem, the temple. If the psalm comes prior to the Babylonian conquest, it could refer to any number of temple repair and rejuvenation programs (e.g., 1 Kgs 15:11–15, 2 Kgs 12:4–16, 2 Kgs 22:3–7); or if after, the text could denote the reconstruction of the "house" (temple) under the direction of Zerubbabel and Joshua (Ezra 3:8–13; 5:1–6:18). Again, the point is the same: without the LORD's backing, the project is doomed to failure.

Regardless of how we might identify the particulars, the message of the first scenario is that every human endeavor must rely on the LORD's support for success; failure to gain the LORD's backing will result in a house—of any and every type—that will collapse, leaving all human effort to be "in vain" (1a)

The second scenario pictures the guard, watching by day and especially at night for any potential threat to the community's well-being (1b). Ancient cities depended on their city guards to cry out at the first sign of danger, potentially saving the city (see Ezek 3:16–21). But sounding a familiar theme, once again the poet claims that without the LORD's prior commitment to the city and human reliance on the LORD, the guards are an exercise in human futility ("the guard keeps watch in vain"). What is of first importance is acquiring the LORD's protection, and then relying on the LORD to guard the city.

The third scenario pictures workers, male or female, who are up to work at the crack of dawn and work late into the evening. The poet says they eat "the bread of anxious toil" (2), while "he" (presumably God) "gives sleep to his beloved" (2). The key question, I think, is to ask why? What would cause a person, then or now, to do what the poet describes—to work sixty to seventy hours or more a week? Why? Is it because we think we must, that if we don't the work will not get done— or worse, it will not be done right (meaning, "my way"). Is it because we believe if we aren't there things will fall apart? Why? Is it because we won't be able to pay the bills, or we will not be able to afford the things we believe we need or want?

I think if we ask ourselves the right question and are honest with ourselves, the answer is not that difficult. House-building, guard-setting, and work habits are merely easy places to look for symptoms of a person, a family, a church, or a nation that relies on itself. With the stroke of a writer's quill the first two verses come together and indict me. With all my heart I do not want to rely on someone else—to open a door for me, help me get my chair up a slope, or drive me to a speaking appointment. I want to be in control.

But I'm not and neither are you. And for me, these are among the most difficult words I've had to learn and relearn *After Lament*. Truth be told, I wasn't in control before my nervous system went haywire; but back then I could fool myself on a routine basis. I could work twelve-hour days, building a university academic department and keeping it running. *After Lament* I am learning that all human efforts and hopes depend on God, not us.

Part II: After careful reading of verses 1–2, the relationship of verses 3–5 to the beginning of the psalm—and the unity of the psalm—is easier to see. Verses 3–5 provide a fourth scenario of the LORD's blessing in a situation we sometimes think we control, but do not. Just ask those who have lamented their ability to get pregnant, or who miscarry one pregnancy after another—the blessing of children is precisely that, a blessing, a gift of God. In Psalm 127 the blessing, is the gift of sons. In years to come these sons will provide strength behind their father as he stands in court (the city gate) arguing with his enemies. A man who has a quiver full of sons, who may be carrying their own quiver full of arrows, will not be pushed around by his opponents.

For some, after their laments Psalm 127 will have no special meaning. Not every wisdom psalm fits every situation *After Lament*. But for others the theme of Psalm 127 will ring true with a clarity they did not and perhaps could not hear prior to their lament. Hannah, after years of disappointment and lament, became pregnant and then presented her only son to the LORD. She knew better than anyone else around that

> Sons are indeed a heritage from the LORD,
>> the fruit of the womb a reward. (Ps 127:5)

Just as she knew that

> Unless the LORD builds the house,
>> those who build it labor in vain. (127:1)

The danger we face is our own growing knowledge and expertise in engineering and constructing high-rise condominiums, sophisticated military defense systems, and medical advances that lead us to believe we are in control. Only when towers collapse, defense systems fail, and medical procedures disappoint do we realize that we are not in control of our world—and we never were.

Psalm 133, the next to last psalm in the "Songs of Ascents" (Ps 120–134), is a deceptively simple meditation on the virtues of unity. The first sentence presents a proverb-like wisdom saying, translated here more literally than in the NRSV:

> Behold, how good and how pleasant,
>> when brothers dwell (sit) together in unity. (133:1)

Short is not simple. Working carefully with the text, two key questions arise: 1) Who are the "brothers" (*'akhim*)? And 2) What are they doing? The two questions and their solutions are interrelated. Of many proposed interpretations, two proposals seem most likely: a) the "brothers" are literal brothers or family members living together on the family's ancestral land, or b) the "brothers" are the members of Israel coming together to worship the LORD (Psalm 133 is a "Psalm of Ascent"). It is difficult to decide between the two options, and I'm not sure we need to choose. Both a family living together in unity and Israel coming together as a family to worship are the subject of verse 1. And in both cases the achievement of togetherness is described as "good" (*tob*), as in when God looked over each day's work of creation and declared it to be "good" (Gen 1:10, 12, 18, 21, 25), and "pleasant" (*na'im*), as in the friendship of David and Jonathan (2 Sam 1:26), the compliments of the lovers in the Song of Songs (1:16, 7:7), or the description of God:

> Praise the LORD, for the LORD is good (*tob*);
>> Sing to his name, for he is gracious (*na'im*). (Ps 135:3)

In Psalm 133 the beauty of unity is further described by two extended metaphors, both of which challenge our understanding because of their distance from us in time and culture. First, unity is . . .

> . . . like the precious oil on the head,
>> running down upon the beard,
> on the beard of Aaron,
>> running down over the collar of his robes. (133:2)

I dare to venture that the image fails to capture our imagination of beauty—this person needs to wash their hair, trim their beard to a modest length (or apply for a role on Duck Dynasty), and clean their robes. In my culture the only time people pour things on others' heads is when they win some championship and are celebrating with champagne in the locker room. But oil? Pouring so much oil on my head that it runs down into my beard, and then from my beard onto my clothes—the beauty is beyond me.

Erich Zenger's work is helpful: "The perfumed oil with which participants in (secular or cultic [worship]) banquets were anointed as they were greeted. . . . [oil] was used especially because of its beguiling, sweet smell" (*Psalms III*, 479). In this case, the host in Psalm 133 goes overboard, pouring so much oil that it flows down the head, down the beard, onto the collar of the robes—a luxurious, lavish, and festive welcome to the party or to worship. The metaphor, however, does not stop here; the writer specifies that all of this is happening "on the beard of Aaron," the first High Priest, whose name stands for all those to come after. Just as verse one causes us to think of the family and then Israel, so this image of oil appeals to us in two ways: a lavish welcome to festive worship, and a vivid reminder of the beautiful rituals in anointing the High Priest.

The second extended metaphor is somewhat simpler and yet equally baffling. Unity is good and pleasant:

> It is like the dew of Hermon,
>> which falls on the mountains of Zion.
> For there the LORD ordained his blessing,
>> life forevermore. (133:3)

A good many interpreters call attention to the heavy dew that falls on Mt. Hermon, and so explain the line "which falls on the mountains of Zion" as a claim about the life-giving qualities that come to or emit from Mt. Zion. Mt. Hermon is in the far north of Canaan, so perhaps these lines intend some comment about the unification of the North and South. Or, most likely, we are to recall that Mt. Hermon was the traditional home to the gods of Canaan, similar to Mt. Olympus in Greek mythology. Thus, verse 3 is a theological correction of sorts: life-giving dew falls on Zion (the home of Yahweh), not Mt. Hermon. As a pilgrimage song, the psalm praises the objective of their travel. Unity is life-giving dew that falls from the home of the true God.

No lament pushes its reader directly toward the instruction found in Psalm 133, though those who have lamented division in their family, church, community, or nation will find particular meaning here. For the rest of us Psalm 133 extols the goodness and beauty of human unity and evokes our sense of sight, smell, and place to commend unity. Sometimes

I get the sense that we pat Psalm 133 on the head for being such a good little psalm. And then we return to our fractured lives, though we are unaware how splintered we have become. We have our Red States and Blue States, the wealthy and poor (with the gap between the two increasing more and more), and conservative churches and liberal churches (though every church I visit claims to be in the middle). The first challenge Psalm 133 presents is for us to become aware of just how fractured our lives have become and our own role in causing the fissures (after all, we are all in the middle where the separation takes place).

Psalm 133 does not teach us how to achieve what it proclaims to be wonderful—unless the constant downward motion in the metaphors is not haphazard, but integral to the psalm. The oil flows down the head, down the beard, and the dew falls down on the mountain. The constant downward movement reminds me of the Christ hymn in Philippians 2:

> Who, though he was in the form of God,
>   did not regard equality with God
>   as something to be exploited,
> but emptied himself,
>   taking the form of a slave,
>   being born in human likeness.
> And being found in human form,
>   he humbled himself
>   and became obedient to the point of death—
>   even death on a cross. (Philip 2:6–8)

As in Psalm 133, the motion is down, down, down even to a cross. Paul presents this form of life, this attitude to be taken up by the Philippian church in its own quest for unity (2:3–5). The only way to have a united family, a united church, or a united country is if we stop looking out for what is ours and start giving up what is rightfully mine for the sake of others—an action and attitude that runs against the grain of our individualistic society.

Psalm 32 is the combination of a thanksgiving psalm and an instruction. The song begins with a declaration of blessing or beatitude, followed by four brief teaching units (3–4, 5, 6–7, 8–11). The beatitude or pronouncement of happiness is for those "whose transgression is forgiven" (1); those to whom the LORD "imputes" or reckons no sin— not those who are sinless, and certainly not those acting as if they are sinless (2b). The blessed are the forgiven: those who have rebelled (the fundamental idea of "transgression," *pasha'*, 1a), those who have deliberately missed the target (the idea of "sin," *khata'ah*, 1b), those who have become twisted or crooked ("iniquity," *yakhshov*, 2a), and those who are unreliable ("deceit," *'aon*, 2b; see Limburg, *Psalms*, 103–104)—but who have found forgiveness. Just how the psalmist found forgiveness, and how others may too, is the theme of the four sections of the psalm.

First, for a long time, the poet writes, I tried to keep silent (3–4). Perhaps no one would notice, or perhaps no one would be able to trace the sinful action back to me. There are as many reasons to deny or hide sin as there are sins. Ultimately, only two attitudes cause us to go silent: fear of what others may think, or pride in a public image that might be destroyed. But the good news is that God would not permit the psalmist to live out a lie. What felt like God's hand came down heavy, causing a disease that "wasted away" his body and zapped his strength like the heat of one summer day after another.

Second, the psalmist understood the cause of his suffering, the connection between his sin and his life, and the disaster in his attempt to keep silent. So he quit trying to hide his failures and instead came clean. He confessed and the LORD forgave him (5).

Third, now the poet turns toward teaching others on the basis of his experience (6). "Therefore" others who follow this God should offer prayer when they find themselves in distress. Then the primeval rush of water will not engulf them. The poet confesses his own experience and his confidence in God, who is a hiding place, who preserves from trouble, and surrounds me "with glad cries of deliverance" (6).

Fourth, the psalmist teaches two lessons, again on the basis of his experience (8).

Lesson one:

> Do not be like a horse or a mule, without understanding,
>> whose temper must be curbed with bit and bridle,
>> else it will not stay near you. (9)

The lesson is clear enough and its relationship to the writer's experience transparent: the writer had been like a stubborn mule that needed God to redirect it with bit and bridle so he would confess and follow God.

Lesson two:

> Many are the torments of the wicked,
>> but steadfast love surrounds those who trust in the
>> LORD. (10)

The writer knows from personal experience that the wicked struggle with many "torments" (10), but those who trust in the LORD experience the steadfast love of the LORD. So, the writer concludes:

> Be glad in the LORD and rejoice, O righteous,
>> and shout for joy, all you upright in heart. (11)

Psalm 32 presents itself to us as the words of a person after lament, someone who has fiercely attempted to hide his sin, but finally turned to God for forgiveness. His lament might be something like what we find in Psalm 25, 130, or 51. But now the writer rejoices for his own blessing and realizes his responsibility to reach out to others on the basis of his own experience (e.g., 51:8). Sin is the human condition—our condition. So the issue is not so much if we sin as how we respond to our sin; whether we try to hide our sin so that others are unaware and we look more saintly, or we come clean. The writer of Psalm 32 assures us that any attempt to hide our sin is futile and ultimately harmful to us. Our best path is to confess before a God whose nature is to forgive.

Our final example is **Psalm 73**, the opening psalm to Book III of the Psalter. At this stage in the Psalms, the Davidic monarchy and the nation are locked in an irreversible downslide that will conclude at the end of Book III with the collapse of the monarchy and the kingdom. Book III is dark, with nine laments out of seventeen psalms, including two of the most intense laments in the entire Book of Psalms (88, 89). I suppose at this point of the Psalter it might be easy to get the wrong idea or decide against the initial instruction of Psalm 1: that God blesses the righteous (1:1), while the wicked will be like chaff that the wind blows away (1:4). With what the poet of Psalm 73 has seen—and what we see every day, unless we refuse to look—it is difficult to believe God is still in control.

The psalm opens with confessions. First, a restatement of Psalm 1:1–3 and every other text in the Psalter that asserts the good reign of the LORD: "Truly God is good to the upright, to those who are pure in heart" (73:1). The second confession is bold and honest:

> But as for me, my feet had almost stumbled;
>> my steps had nearly slipped.
> For I was envious of the arrogant;
>> I saw the prosperity of the wicked. (2–3)

Who hasn't felt this way? Other than Job's friends who had spiritual macro-degeneration so they couldn't see what was directly in front of them; who hasn't looked around and seen the affluence of the wicked and wondered with the psalmist—have I chosen wisely? (3)

Anyone who can see—and is willing to look—knows what the poet describes in verses 4–12. The first phrase grabs my attention: *they have no pain (4a).* No, their bodies are "sound and sleek" (4b), escaping whatever bug that might be going around (5) and eating well every day (7). They may not all have the looks of Angelina Jolie or Brad Pitt; but they are not Michael J. Fox with a disease (Parkinsons) that keeps them from doing what they love to do or Patrick Swayze who dies young from pancreatic cancer. "They are not plagued like other people" (5b). So they put on pride like a necklace (6a), and why not? Every indicator suggests they are better than other people; and such a position makes it easy for them to look down on others—and they do. They can threaten the little people with immunity and erupt with a violent temper as easy as putting on a shirt (6a). They are always at ease, with money pouring in (12). And the little people (everyone else) watch them and heap more praise on them; they are our stars. And about the only thing they have to say about God is who needs him or her? (9)—if indeed there is a God who can see, much less do anything to us (11).

Tell me you don't know, directly or indirectly, such people. And tell me that you haven't wondered, like this poet, what's the point of trying so hard to serve the LORD with a holy life when all the goods go to people whose only words for God are "Bug off." Meanwhile, I feel as if God punishes me every morning, every day I step out of bed into pain (14). If this is the way it is going to be, then what's the point? Why bother? And it is at this point that the poet catches himself. I know my descriptions of God and life with God are over-drawn and unfair (15). And yet, that does not mean the poet or we can stop thinking—and buy another bumper sticker to plaster over the problem and fix everything: "Hey, Don't Worry, Depend on Jesus," or "When you make God bigger, your problems become smaller." Gee, thanks a lot; that solves every-thing. Everyone must come to you for spiritual counseling. Except the poet of Psalm 73; he keeps thinking, even if it is wearisome (16). And he goes to the sanctuary (17) and there, somehow, finds the answers he needs.

It is much easier to see the answers the poet found (18–28) than to understand how the poet arrived at these conclusions (17). So we begin with the three answers. First, the poet discovers that the "end" of the prosperous wicked will come without warning, in the flash of a moment, without their memory or fame left to remember (18–20). Second, the poet recognizes that his rant (in verses 4–14) was stupid and ignorant (21–22); but even then he knows that "I am continually with you; you hold my right hand" (23). Despite the writer's frustration, God was not going anywhere. And for that matter, neither is the poet about to leave his God:

> You guide me with your counsel,
>> and afterward you will receive me with honor.
> Whom have I in heaven but you?
>> And there is nothing on earth that I desire other
>> than you.
> My flesh and heart may fail,
>> but God is the strength of my heart and my portion
>> forever. (24–26)

Their relationship is strong enough that honest words are no threat to their bond. Richard Clifford observes that the visit to the temple "does not alter the situation; the wicked are still carefree and the righteous are still afflicted. Rather, the new understanding makes it possible to bear these afflictions, for God is now recognized to be there" (Clifford, *Psalms 73–150*, 19).

Third, putting both lessons together, the poet is reminded that those "far from you will perish; you put an end to those who are false to you" (27); and I know that for me it is best to be near God. "I have made the LORD my refuge" (28b). The path to reaffirmation of faith in God's justice and confirmation of my relationship to God has taken some sharp turns and some hard words, but anything less would cheapen the relationship.

As for how the psalmist came back to the orthodoxy of his faith, the easiest and perhaps best answer is that we do not know. In verses 4–16 everything is upside-down and understanding "this . . . seemed to me a wearisome task" (16b). But then the poet went into the sanctuary (temple?), and when he comes out, while nothing is yet resolved, he has the answers he needs ("I perceived their end" [17b]). Proposals abound as to what happened in the sanctuary: the poet engaged in worship which reminded him of the core values of his faith (Limburg,

247; Grogan, 134; Terrien, *The Psalms,* 531), he received a revelation from God in which the poet "perceived their end" (17b; Clifford, *Psalms 73–150,* 18; Kraus, *Psalms 60–150,* 89), he had an experience of God "'as a sanctuary,' that is, as saving, protecting, and joy-bringing closeness" (Zenger, *Psalms 2,* 232), the poet (a sage) meditated in the presence of the LORD until he remembered what was genuine or true about this world (Mays, 242–243), or perhaps the writer received a prophetic oracle that reassured him of God's plans (Tate, *Psalms 51–100,* 238, among other possible explanations). Which of these took place in the sanctuary to help the poet re-emerge with assurance in God's presence and justice, in my opinion, is anyone's guess.

Psalm 73 is for those who have realized (in their lament?) that the faith claims of their religion do not always match up to their experience, and who, as a result, nearly give up on God. It is a situation faced by Israel in her destruction and exile, by Job as the result of a petty wager between the Satan and God, and by the faithful of every generation. Sooner or later we find ourselves in need of an experience in the temple, whatever that may turn out to be for you—worship with the community, solitary meditation, or some other experience in which we learn that what is most important is God, not what God gives or God withholds from me or from others: "there is nothing on earth that I desire other than you" (73:25b). Claus Westermann adds:

> Others, like the author of Job or Psalm 73, realized that this doctrine did not correspond to reality, and from this arose a completely different, and wholly new, attitude: one must hold fast to God and continue to trust Him even when one no longer understands what He is doing. (Westermann, *The Living Psalms,* 145)

In Psalm 73, at the center of the Psalter stands a psalm with lessons critical for every person who has ever emerged *After Lament* without the results he or she hoped for.

- Even when I was embittered, "you hold my right hand" (23b). God did not walk or run away from my complaint.
- When all is said and done, "there is nothing on earth I desire other than you [God]" (25b)
- Ultimately, "God is the strength of my heart" (26b) and "for me it is good to be near God" (28a)

Critical lessons, but the most difficult lessons I've ever had to learn, wrestling with them over and over again. So please do not rush into the hospital room of a friend in pain and tell her you have the lessons she needs to learn from her experience.

Conclusion

In this chapter we have followed a small group of laments that direct their readers toward God's instruction *After Lament*. And while we cannot know the specific instruction these laments have in mind, the four sample wisdom psalms we have studied make especially good sense if or when they are considered after a related lament.

- Psalm 127 stresses the futility of human effort without the LORD's blessing.
- Psalm 133 praises the virtue of unity in the home, the nation, and all other groups.
- Psalm 32 gives thanks for forgiveness and provides instruction for others on the basis of the psalmist's experience.
- Psalm 73 talks the reader through the devastating realization that comes when faith claims do not match lived experience.

The common theme of these four examples is a fundamental trust or reliance on the LORD: to bless our work, to unify our fractured lives, to forgive when we risk confession, and do what is in our best interest, especially when we do not understand or like what God is doing. From where I sit this morning, after my own lament for pain that will not go away and all the losses that have come with the pain, learning to trust God again is without doubt the challenge of my life.

During lament I'm not sure we are capable of hearing any of these psalms, e.g., for someone to storm in and teach us what we need to learn from our time in disorientation; and we are certainly not ready for someone to claim they know *why* we are going through difficult times. Those who would minister to the broken need the spiritual gift of patience and self-control. A time to teach may come—*After Lament*, but during lament what is most needed are ears that listen, not a tongue that loves to talk and solve everything. When Job's friends showed up they spent a week just sitting with him on the ground, not speaking a word (Job 2:13); if only they could have kept their mouths shut.

CHAPTER NINE

Spoke #6: Broken Hope

Lament is a language in motion toward hope both in its form and content. In content, lament's hope is manifest in its movement toward thanksgiving, new praise, joy, renewed trust, and even instruction. In form, lament has a natural shape that leads toward a final outburst of praise or confidence for what the LORD will do or perhaps has already done. No matter how awful the circumstances may be, somehow the poets lead us to believe again that we can trust our God to help.

But not always. In chapter three we described lament as a wagon wheel with spokes that represented the various directions in which groups of laments lead their readers (e.g., thanksgiving, new praise, joy), all within the unifying presence of trust. But we also recognized another group of laments comprising another spoke that is, in some fashion, broken. Just how broken the spoke may be—how broken our hope may be—varies with each psalm. It may be that the spoke has broken off the axle and rim or it might still be more or less attached. As we look more closely at these psalms, it will become clear that our hope depends on our trust. In laments that lead their readers to thanksgiving, hope soars for what we believe God is about to do. But in laments that struggle to find reasons to trust God, to believe God cares, much less will do anything, our hope sputters down the runway like an old minivan trying to take flight. Lost trust leaves us grounded, wondering, searching, even hoping for reasons to believe again.

Lost hope is devastating. I know. I know what is like to lose hope that a marriage can ever come back to life. And I know what it feels like to finally admit to myself that I was at the end of what conventional medicine could do for my pain; to accept that for the rest of my life every morning I was going to wake up, put my feet on the ground, and begin another day in pain. Some days my tools (including medicine) will help, and other days nothing helps. And there is no rhyme or reason to predict what the rest of today, much less what tomorrow will hold.

But some of you know better than me about lost hope; you've heard the diagnoses from which there is no recovery, just the question: how long? The unexpected phone call or highway patrol officer at your front door in the middle of the night. The ways hope can be snatched, shot, or destroyed are more than I could ever list. I suppose if the sky were a scroll and the sea was ink, even then the sky could not contain all the ways in which hope may be lost. And here we may begin to see the critical difference between hope and trust; how it is possible to trust God, even if we have lost hope in the present circumstances. We will return to this idea later in the chapter.

Nonetheless, lament is a language that by its nature leads toward trust and hope. But there are exceptions, and these exceptions are our focus here: the laments that do not urge their readers toward thanksgiving, new praise, renewed joy, or even the slightest instruction. I mentioned three examples in chapter three (Pss 38, 88, 137), and wrote about Psalms 44, 88, and 89 in *Hurting with God*. Here, however, we need to return to some of these psalms in order to think about them from the perspective of this book. Where do we go and what do we do *after* these laments? What do we do with the disappointment inscribed into these psalms—and into our lives?

Four Laments

Walter Brueggemann describes **Psalm 88** as "an embarrassment to conventional faith" (*Message of the Psalms*, 78), and he is on target. The psalm begins and ends in darkness (88:1, 18); no movement has taken place or is envisioned as taking place, except that the writer's life is getting closer and closer to the grave (3), so close that others already count him among the dead (4). Still there might be hope if not for the fact that God is the one who is killing him (6) because God is so inexplicably angry (7). The poet reaches out day after day to God, but there is no help (4b), and no response (9–10, 13). Meanwhile, God has also taken away the poet's friends, those who might have extended some measure of comfort (8).

Why God has decided to throw a servant into a grave makes no sense to the psalmist (11–12, 14)—or to me. But that is exactly what God is doing. What's worse, God has been beating the psalmist, taking out divine anger on him for as long as the poet can remember (15–17), sending one wave of assault after another. And despite the poet's prayers every evening (1–2) and morning (3), the LORD refuses to answer, as if he is too busy planning the next terrible thing to do to the psalmist.

I would argue that for Psalm 88 hope has been pulverized by God's relentless attacks—and there is little hope that God is going to change any time soon, if ever. And yet, on some level trust remains in this God who refuses to answer, night and day, again and again, because the psalmist continues to pray to this God night and day, again and again. But just where are we supposed to go with God when Psalm 88 describes our lives? When it is one of the ten wonders of faith that this poet and we continue to pray, what do we do after our prayer—*After Lament*?

The author of **Psalm 39** did his best not to say anything. He didn't want to slip-up and say the wrong thing and he didn't want to give the wicked ammunition they could turn against God-followers (39:1). But most of all he knew what he would have to say if he spoke at all.

So he held his tongue, bit his tongue, and stood on his tongue—but he couldn't do it. He could not run a Watergate cover-up and keep what God was doing secret, not even for God. The more he thought about it, the more it burned him up (2–3). So he blew the whistle because people needed to know the truth. First, in comparison to his own existence, God has made human life incredibly short, so short that God might not even notice his life; it is only the breath-vapor on a cold morning—blink and you miss it (4–5). But people don't understand, because if they did they would not be running all around in turmoil trying to get stuff that they will hold for only an instant before they die and it goes to someone else (6).

Second, God beats people up, even when they confess their sin (8–10). Again the poet reminds us that at one point he was silent, not saying a thing about God's activities. But God kept beating him up anyway; so what's the point in not blowing the whistle if "I am worn down by the blows of your hand" (10b) either way I go. And it's not just me; everyone is beneath the hand of a God who punishes them and takes away the very things they have collected to give their short lives some meaning and joy.

So the writer of Psalm 39 makes two unusual requests. 1) "I am a passing guest, an alien like my ancestors"—a statement that veils a subtle appeal to the LORD's own laws requiring Israel to extend kindness toward aliens. Israel was forbidden to do what the LORD is doing to this poet. Instead, Israel was to love the alien as herself (Lev 19:33–34). Surely the God of Justice will adhere to his own principles and quit oppressing his passing guests on earth (12). 2) Or, if that doesn't work, then stop looking at me. Leave me alone so that I have a chance to smile again before I die (13).

At the center of this psalm there is a baffling confession.

> And now, O LORD, what do I wait for?
> My hope is in you. (39:7)

The poet's statement and request sounds like abused children who, despite the abuse, cry out for the parent who abused them. Just what does a whistle-blower do with God *after* blowing the whistle on God?

Because of their similarities, we may consider **Psalm 44** and **Psalm 89** together. Neither of these psalms conclude with hopeful praise or confidence for what the Lord will do for them. Instead, Psalm 44 begs the Lord to wake up (44:23), stop hiding his face (24, compare to Num 6:24–26), and come to our help on account of his steadfast love (44:25–26). In the same way, Psalm 88 concludes by asking God how long he intends to hide himself, with his anger burning like fire (88:46). The poet also asks where God's steadfast love has gone—because it certainly isn't around here anymore (88:49); God should consider what his servant is suffering every day because of God (88:50–51). Unanswered requests for help conclude these psalms, not joyful praise or confident trust in what God will do for them.

These psalms also begin alike, with reminders to the reader/hearer and to God about the Lord's once faithful love. In Psalm 44 the reminder is of God's hand driving out the peoples of the promised land and planting Israel in their place (44:1–3); and a memo to God of how much the writer's community still trusts in God and his salvation (44:4–8). In Psalm 89 the psalmist's declaration of the Lord's steadfast love encompasses 37 verses and covers at least two topics: 1) the Lord's powerful reign over all other gods, creation, and his own people (1–2, 5–18), and 2) the selection of and covenant with David and his family for an eternal dynasty (3–4, 19–37).

Finally, both psalms make explicit accusations against the Lord, accusations that are apt to take our breath away. In Psalm 44 the poet accuses the Lord of not accompanying Israel's troops into battle (44:9), with the consequences of a massive defeat in which the Lord "made us like sheep for slaughter" (44:11a) and Israel being scattered among the nations (11b). The Lord sold out his people for nothing (12). And God has utterly shamed his people, making them the joke of the ancient Near East (13–16). The Lord has done all these things, and yet:

> we have not forgotten you,
>> or been false to your word.
> Our heart has not turned back,
>> nor have our steps departed from your way. (44:17–18)

We are innocent. We did not deserve what God has done to us (20–21), but even so

> Because of you we are being killed all day long,
>> and accounted as sheep for the slaughter. (44:22)

God is at fault, but we are the one's paying for God's injustice. So, at the very least, God should wake up and get to work fixing what he has done (23–26).

Psalm 89 is no less explicit or demanding. The poet accuses the LORD of renouncing the eternal covenant he made with the dynasty of David (89:38–39, cf. 89:21, 28–29, 33–37). Like Psalm 44, the writer accuses God of not supporting the king in battle, with the consequence of massive destruction in the throne city (40–43). God has done exactly what he promised he would never do.

The Promise:
> His line shall continue forever,
>> and his throne endure before me like the sun. (89:36)

The Betrayal:
> You have removed the scepter from his hand,
>> and hurled his throne to the ground. (89:44)

And while the poet does not claim innocence, neither does he accept guilt that would justify what God has done. Instead, he reminds God that the covenant with David's dynasty was supposed to last regardless of human failure (30–34). So here, as in Psalm 44, the poet indicts and holds the LORD guilty of covenant breaking.

Other psalms might be added to these psalms in which hope in the present circumstances has been lost and trust in the LORD, to one degree or another, has been broken (see also Pss 60, 80, 90). In fact, the amazing thing about all of these psalms is that despite their loss of hope in the present situation and their charges against God for divine failures ranging from neglect and abuse (Ps 88), assault (Ps 39), desertion in battle (Ps 44), to covenant breaking (Ps 89)—despite these charges, trust has not been lost. In the words of Psalm 39, even though the Lord is to blame for the massive defeat, with God's people like sheep going to the slaughter, the poet still writes,

> And now, O Lord, what do I wait for?
> My hope is in you. (39:7)

Some measure of faith or trust remains for each of these psalmists, otherwise they would not pray to the Lord, especially not in a manner that seeks to save the relationship.

After Lament

Where do we go from here? These laments do not lead us toward any of the typical responses (e.g., thanksgiving, new praise, joy, trust, instruction) or any response at all. These are broken laments; like broken wheels they do not move us forward as we expect. Psalm 88 begins and ends in darkness. Psalm 39 begins in silence and concludes asking God to turn his gaze away so the writer may be able to smile again. And Psalms 44 and 89 start with memories of God's faithfulness and end with desperate requests for God's faithfulness to return. What can be done with broken spokes?

1. Letting My Hope Die

Sometimes broken laments exist to let the present hope die in order for us to accept a new future. In other words, God says no to the lament so we will move in a different direction; thus, God replaces one spoke for another to change our expectations or hopes for the future. In 2 Corinthians 12 Paul provides an example of such a broken lament. Paul tells his readers, "a thorn was given me in the flesh, a messenger of

Satan to torment me" (2 Cor 12:7). So far as I am aware, New Testament scholars have not reached any consensus on what Paul's thorn in the flesh actually was—if it matters. From my perspective (naturally), it sounds like something painful. But it remains open like the ambiguous identity of the enemies in the laments.

What we do know is that Paul did not like or want the "thorn" and appealed to God three times to remove it (2 Cor 12:8). The picture here is not Paul praying once, twice, three times and that's the end of his appeal. Rather "three times" is a way of saying completely or fully. Paul prayed about the thorn until it was clear to him that the answer to his prayer was "No." Instead of getting what he hoped for, his prayer of lament led to God's words: "My grace is sufficient for you, for power is made perfect in weakness" (2 Cor 12:8). From our perspective Paul's lament failed to get rid of something that was holding back his work; but that's not the way God saw it. God needed Paul to give up or let go of the object of his prayers—his hope—so that God could do something else with his life. Paul never gave up his trust in God, but his hope for a "thornless" life had to go.

In the same way, Jesus prays three times in the garden, "My Father, if it is possible, let this cup pass from me; yet not what I want but what you want" (Matt 26:39–44). Jesus' prayer/lament also failed to achieve its objective; but that does not mean that Jesus lost trust in the Father. It does mean, however, that after his vigorous attempts to convince the Father of some other plan, it was time for Jesus to give up his hope in exchange for where God was leading him.

There have been few times in my life when I have prayed "three times" and eventually realized I needed to let that hope die in order to accept what God was wanting to do in my life. Perhaps I have expected far too little of God, or maybe I have been incredibly blessed. But I know that I have reached (and passed) the point at which I needed to give up the lament for my "thorn," to allow my hope for no more pain to die, so that I could move toward whatever future God might have for my life in light of my new circumstances.

Was this decision easy? Absolutely not!

How did I know? I'm not sure. But after four or five years of broken lament, I began to get a clue that God's answer was no. And at the same time I began to get a sense of where God was trying to lead me. Perhaps a new ministry in writing with fewer physical demands (*Let the reader decide*). That's not to say I am sure. Often, it is only after the benefit of many years that we are able to look back and see what God was doing in our lives. And that's not to say that I still don't have days in which I beg for greater pain relief. But I do know that acceptance of my condition has enabled me to move ahead, instead of constant frustration and chasing one physician after another hoping for what does not exist. Acceptance has meant working with a team of medical specialists to give me the best relief possible with a mind sharp enough to still teach and write; and getting a great wheel chair to use for long "walks" and time I would otherwise have to stand.

So, some broken laments may be telling us that it is time to give up on a hope, painful as it may be, and begin looking ahead to God's new leading. Just how long you (and others on your behalf) are to pray before you know that you have reached "three times," I can't tell you. You might want to consult pastors and others with wisdom. But giving up on some hope does not mean you are giving up on God; in fact, a dashed hope given over to God can be a tremendous act of faith.

2. Continue to Pray with Persistence

On the other hand, just because God has yet to respond to our prayer does not necessarily mean we should give up our hope and quit praying. As a general rule, we do not wait well. We do not exercise patience or persistence, and we are apt to give up too quickly and then blame God for dashing our hopes against the rocks.

We need to hear a different text from the New Testament, which begins: "Then Jesus told them a parable about their need to pray always *and not to lose heart*" (Luke 18:1, emphasis mine). In the story are two characters: a widow with a need for justice, and a judge "who neither feared God nor had respect for people" (18:2). The widow kept coming to the judge and asking for justice in regard to her opponent—over and over and over again. Eventually, even though the judge did not care about her, her case, or justice, he decided to grant her justice simply so "she not wear me out by continually coming" (18:5). Jesus concludes: "will not God grant justice to his chosen ones who cry to him day and night? Will he delay long in helping them? I tell you, he will quickly grant justice to them" (18:7-8a).

For those of us who are apt to give up and throw in the towel at the first sign of difficulty, we need to hear Paul's words of encouragement: "Pray without ceasing" (1 Thes 5:17), "persevere in prayer" (Rom 12:12), and "Pray in the Spirit at all times in every prayer and supplication. To that end keep alert and always persevere in supplication for all the saints" (Eph 6:18). And Jesus' assurance, "So I tell you, whatever you ask for in prayer, believe that you have received it, and it will be yours" (Mark 11:24; see also Matt 18:19, John 14:13–14, 15:7). We should not give up too quickly; but with confidence in God we should pray persistently, even turning to others who have greater confidence in what God can and will do (see Mark 9:28–29, James 5:13–18).

Returning to our metaphor of the wagon wheel and broken spokes, some spokes (laments) have been tossed aside and regarded as unfit because we have given up hope too quickly in what God can do. Why God delays and doesn't answer our lament the first time we pray is beyond my wisdom. It could be that we are not yet ready for what we pray (even though we think we are) or others are not ready. Perhaps God has some other plan that is larger and more important, and that requires the sacrifice of my hope. Or maybe God has some side bet with the Satan about how persistent we will be in our prayer or how faithful we will be if we don't get what we want (see Job 1:8–12, 2:3–6). I don't know—and I am certain that's best.

All I can say is that in an age of super-fast customer service and immediate gratification of our desires, the spiritual discipline of persistent prayer is rare; whether that prayer is lament, thanksgiving, or praise. And so, too many 'spokes' of lament lay discarded because we gave up too soon, and left our hopes to rot; when for reasons known to God alone, we needed to keep praying.

3. Accept and Help within a New Normal

Options one and two for dealing with the broken spokes in laments such as Psalms 88, 39, 44, and 89 only go a short distance in explaining why these laments have lost hope and, more important, *how we respond to help*. These two answers are equally unsatisfactory when we are talking about a lament for a child dying of leukemia or a young mother dying of cancer. I am unwilling to accept the idea that for God's kingdom to move forward, either the child or mother must die. Did we not pray persistently enough or without enough faith in God's ability? Did we need fifty more faithful saints? A hundred? I am confident that the poets of Psalm 88, 39, 44, and 89 would offer their hearty "Amen" to my objection.

So what are we to make of all these other broken spokes, laments in which hope for God's help has been lost? To move forward, I must first confess fears that surround our conversation.

a) I fear any solution that reduces the LORD to a candy machine: put my money in the slot (pray), operate the buttons correctly (have faith), and get what I want. All we need is to learn how to "handle" God so that he performs on time and we get what we want. So let me state this clearly: *God is not a coin-operated machine that dispenses goods for payment.*

b) I also fear reducing our expectations of God so much that we put God into hibernation, where he is alive but not functioning. Or in different terms, the LORD is on the inactive roster for the duration of the season. So any prayer that happens to be answered is really just a stroke of luck, because I don't think God is doing much, if anything in the world today. So let me state this clearly too: *God is alive and well, and intimately involved with his creation.*

c) I also fear that solutions one (giving up hope for new hope) and two (persist, don't give up so easily) may both be misunderstood as simplistic solutions ready for printing on tee shirts and bumper stickers. I've been able to hear these messages from those who have experienced lost hope, those who knew what it was like to hold on to hope with their last ounce of energy. These believers knew what my experience was like, and how complicated and paradoxical life can be. So let me state this clearly also: *These solutions cannot be reduced to gimmicks printed on T-shirts and bumper stickers.*

So with these fears out in the open, we may consider a third strategy regarding broken spokes and dashed hopes. Occasionally a student will meet me on campus and ask if she might lay her hands on me and pray; these students have beautiful hearts and the best of intentions, and I believe in prayer (see above). But in my case, they are coming into my story late and don't understand how important it is for me to accept my new "normal." What I need most are prayers that accept my new normal and ask for me to have the strength to live through this day faithfully with pain, not prayers for healing. I often permit the student to go ahead, or thank her for the concern and ask her to pray elsewhere at another time.

These students illustrate both a problem and a potential for helping those dealing with broken laments that have life-long consequences. I have some friends who affirm this point from a different perspective. Their son was born with significant and obvious disabilities. In response many believers prayed for a miracle that year and the next (and the next), but a miracle failed to come. In addition to communal prayers, many individuals would approach the Smiths (not their real name) and ask if they might lay hands on and pray for Steven (not his real name). After some time the Smiths realized that such prayer was not helpful to their need to accept the reality of the situation and their new normal. So they began to ask those who approached them *to stop praying* for healing in their presence; if they wanted to pray a healing prayer—fine. Just don't do it around us and don't tell us about it. In response, some were confused, others felt hurt, and some judged the Smiths harshly for their lack of faith.

The Smiths did not lack faith; they had a strong, resilient faith that was able to identify and accept when God's answer was "No." Instead of healing, God called them to live out faith with broken hopes for their son and his life—and their own. So what they needed were not healing prayers, but people who were willing to walk alongside them into an unknown future. Amid broken lament, prayer is nice; but other actions can be much better. In fact, *prayer can be the easiest and least thing* for a Christian to do. Prayer can be the equivalent of an impersonal Christian cop-out: "We prayed for you last week"—though we had no idea what you really needed or what we might actually have done to help.

Now to be fair, we Christians, like physicians, have not been well-trained in what to do with cases in which the patient doesn't get better, when the illness is chronic, or even terminal. I know that until I found my present medical team, other doctors were unsure of what to do with me; should they write me off as a mental case or an addict looking to score some easy drugs? In the same way, believers are used to reading the prayer list, praying, and seeing those people back in church within the next Sunday or two—perhaps even celebrating an incredible act of God in saving and healing someone from a terrible car accident. We must learn to acknowledge and celebrate the incredible faith and stamina of those to whom God said no and yet maintain faith.

What the Smiths needed were those who would help, not just pray; people to walk with them in acceptance of this broken lament. Taking turns caring for Steven in church so that the Smiths could worship together. Providing nights of relief so the Smiths could go out or just stay home and rest. And when Steven was in the hospital again (and again), along with the prayers, lift up some money to help with the staggering hospital bills. And most important, not run away when this journey became frightening and overwhelming—because the Smiths couldn't run away. This level of Christian care and commitment is not necessarily better than prayer, but it may well be the answer to prayer.

4. Balance: Praise While We Lament

Not all of the psalmists predicate their actions on the basis of God's favorable response to their lament. In some cases the writers are determined to respond to God in a positive manner no matter what. For example, some of the laments that lead their readers toward praise do so regardless of the Lord's decision. And in a similar, but weaker fashion, two laments that encourage joy do so no matter what may come of their appeal. In both cases, for the writers leading toward praise and joy, their laments are not totally without hope. Hope remains to one degree or another that God will help. But before their cases are resolved, these believers show us how it is possible to engage in praise and rejoicing before the Lord while we are also engaged in vigorous lament.

We find a similar practice among other broken spokes. For example, Psalm 88 begins with what at first appears to be an innocent and common statement: "O Lord, God of my salvation" (88:1a). But in view of the darkness that follows (88:1b-18b), this statement is a remarkable testimony to faith. Psalm 89 begins with more developed testimony:

> I will sing of your steadfast love, O Lord, forever;
> > with my mouth I will proclaim your faithfulness to
> all generations.
> > I declare that your steadfast love is established forever;
> > your faithfulness is as firm as the heavens. (89:1–2)

Of course, the writer of Psalm 89 also uses most of the psalm to describe God's past faithfulness (3–37), even though these verses are a set-up for the accusations at the end of the psalm (38–51).

My point is that even with a broken spoke, a lament that has little or no reason for hope, it is still possible to praise and rejoice in the Lord. Admittedly, we do not often find such words when hope is lost (a spoke is broken) and I confess that in Psalm 89 the praise is a set-up for the complaint. Nonetheless, we do find testimony to abiding trust and worship in the laments struggling to find hope.

What this means, I think, is that even a harsh lament need not swallow us alive so that we do nothing but think about our problems and lament. We should lament—but we should also praise the LORD who reigns. After I returned from the Baylor Pain Management Program I bought a plaque that I hung in my bedroom as a daily reminder:

> Life isn't about waiting for the storm to pass.
> It's about learning to Dance in the Rain.

Taken alone, lament can consume our lives—and our churches. So our last point is about balance and praise—in prayer and song. In the midst of continued lament we need the practice of praise.

Conclusion

Lost hope can be devastating, as we grieve the death of our plans and dreams for the future and face a new "normal" to which we must adjust our lives. But as we have seen in this chapter, while hope in the present may be lost, that does not mean we have lost faith in God. Certainly our trust may be shaken, and we will wonder why the LORD refused to respond to our lament. But as the Psalms testify, hope and trust are not the same; we may hope for many things in our prayers, but our trust in the LORD supersedes our hope.

Those whose lives cannot be described without including the story of some significant lost hope that challenged their faith and sent their lives spinning in a different direction than they had planned, these are my faith heroes. I am glad to join the church celebrating some wonderful act of God—just as we prayed: when God works a great healing or some other wonderful reversal. But my faith heroes are those who have suffered the loss of a spoke (or two) off the wagon wheel; their hope has been devastated, and yet they continue to walk by faith within the new normal created by the loss of hope.

I asked readers of my website to help me identify the people of faith that they admire: spouses of those with Alzheimer's disease who care for the one they love day after day, parents who raise children with disabilities, one who is at the bedside of his comatose spouse every day, and grandparents raising their grandchildren. None of these planned their lives to turn out as it has; their laments failed to gain the blessing they wanted. And yet, despite the loss of hope, they not only still trust the LORD, but live amazing, faith-filled lives.

CHAPTER TEN

After Lament

In the preceding chapters we have followed the spokes of lament to the psalms that come after lament: psalms of trust, thanksgiving psalms, new hymns of praise, psalms that help us rejoice in the Lord, Torah or wisdom psalms, and even broken laments which, as of yet, cannot move forward. We've seen and learned much about what the psalms say and do in the aftermath of lament. But to conclude our study we need to go back to the place we began and see what insights the stories of Job, Abraham and Isaac, and Naomi after their laments may provide us.

1. Job

At the end of the Book of Job, after the lament, God instructs Job with two sizzling speeches that put Job back in his place (as a human). And then the unexpected begins to happen. God tells Job or is asked by his three friends to pray for them because they "have not spoken of me what is right, as my servant Job has" (42:7–8). Those out to protect God (and their theology) at all costs are put in their place, with an assist from the man who would not let God off the hook.

God restores Job's fortune at the rate of double what he had before: sheep, camels, oxen, and donkeys (42:10, 12). I suppose that's nice, but I wonder if Job really cares about these things now. Then "all his brothers and sisters and all who had known him before" come with a donation of money and gold rings for the "Let's Help Job" foundation. They "showed him sympathy and comforted him for all the evil [trouble] that the LORD had brought upon him" (42:11). I can't help but ask: *where in the world have all these people been for the last forty chapters of Job's life?* They know about Job's trouble, but it's not until *after the lament* is over and the trouble resolved that they move in to help; and it's only after the lament that we find out they even exist. They have been watching and waiting to see how things end up before they step in to get involved, when it is safe and there is no danger that they might help the wrong side or lose their reputation by affiliation with the sinner Job. Better not to take sides at all, a safe stance in which we help no one. *Only after lament do they come, and their names are legion.*

Then come the children: once again, seven sons and three daughters—women so beautiful they gain an inheritance along with their brothers (42:13–14) and we even get to know their names (Jemimah, Keziah, Keren-happuch). Sad to say, but women had to gain their identity through physical beauty even in Job's time. His children are no doubt a blessing. But of all that happens to Job (and his wife[s]) this blessing has to be the most bittersweet. Job had ten grown children before the LORD's wager with the Satan took their lives (a wager Job knows nothing about, thank God). But the story teller seems to think that these ten new children, with such exceptional women, will replace the first ten. But they don't; they cannot. Ever.

The book ends with Job beaten, scarred, and in a different place with his God—no matter how much God may give and restore. Job knows too much now; he knows what might happen to a person at any time or place—*for absolutely no reason at all*. He cannot declare thirty-one promises to speak over his life and actually believe these promises will assure his best life now. Or believe that if he sends money to the right evangelist he can find the miracle he has been hoping for. He can never go back, never enjoy the assured stability he once had. *After Lament* he is a changed person. We all are.

2. Abraham and Isaac

We have essentially no information about the relationship between Abraham and Isaac after the near-sacrifice (Gen 22). Sarah dies (Gen 23) and Abraham arranges a marriage for Isaac (Gen 24). Then Abraham dies (Gen 24:7–8) and Isaac and Ishmael bury him in the family tomb, the cave of Machpelah (Gen 24:9). Between the near-sacrifice and Abraham's death, no interaction between Isaac and Abraham is recorded except for the arranged marriage, and even here there is no recorded contact between the father and son.

I am hesitant to make much of this silence. At this stage in Genesis the details of interpersonal relationships are sparse, unlike what will come in the Joseph story (Gen 36–50). Hog-tied, Isaac had no time to lament, as defined by the Psalms. And we have no clue what was going through Abraham's mind (until the New Testament claim in Hebrews 11:17–19). The story is important for us because of the crisis of faith it evokes and how it stirs our imaginations about how one handles such moments. I cannot help but wonder if, in some sense, Abraham sacrificed something of his relationship with his son that day on the mountain. How could a son be tied up with a knife coming to slice his throat and not walk away in a different direction (recall chapter 1), with a changed relationship to his father? And I wonder what he thought of his father's God?

3. Naomi and Ruth

When Naomi returned home from burying her husband and both sons, she didn't want to hear any of the town's stirring. She didn't want to be called "Pleasant" (Naomi), but "Bitter" (Mara) because that is how the Lord treated her. She left full, but the LORD brought her back empty (Ruth 1:20–21). And if we read carefully we see that the mistreatment is not over.

Naomi and Ruth (her deceased son's wife) take desperate measures to ensure their future—"desperate" because the men in the story who should take action to help them do little (Boaz) to nothing (the unnamed relative) to help these women *as they should*. Naomi and Ruth have to force the men into doing what should have been done to help them when they arrived back home. The next of kin should marry Ruth and take care of these women; but not until Boaz is pushed (3:1–13) and the nearest of kin is put on the spot (4:1–8) does anyone take responsibility. Then, and only then, does the story have a "happy" but strange ending.

When Ruth bears a child, the women of the town are eager to praise the Lord for helping Naomi: "Blessed be the Lord, who has not left you this day without next-of-kin; and may his name be renowned in Israel!" (4:14) But I notice that Naomi and Ruth do not appear to be any part of this worship and praise gathering. The men in the story are strutting about as if helping these women had been their idea, their initiative (4:9–12). And while Naomi gets her grandson, Ruth disappears from her own story (4:13–17).

4. Boston and West

Let's bring our stories and reflections closer to home, in both time and proximity. For most of us the week of April 14–20, 2013 has probably already begun to fall through the cracks of our memory, unless you live in Boston or the small community of West, Texas. In which case, depending on your proximity to the events and the people, life now has a new and permanent *before and after* marker: *before* April 15, 2013, ~3:00 PM Eastern Standard Time *and after*, four hours into the Boston City Marathon when two brothers allegedly decided to rain their terror on the marathon and the city of Boston, and *before* April 17, 2013, 7:53 PM Central Standard Time *and after* when the fertilizer plant in West, already burning, exploded in a massive fire ball that registered 2.1 on the Richter scale.

Before and after moments are points along the way that help define our lives, from birth and giving birth until death. Sometimes we are fully in control, enacting important decisions we have prayed over, thought out, and are ready to take (like Abraham with Isaac?). Other times we have no more control than the crowd near the finish line of the marathon. We were at the wrong place at the wrong time. The Preacher had it right years ago:

> the race is not to the swift, nor the battle to the strong, nor bread to the wise, nor riches to the intelligent, nor favor to the skillful; but time and chance happen to them all. For no one can anticipate the time of disaster. Like fish taken in a cruel net, and like birds caught in a snare, so mortals are snared at a time of calamity, when it suddenly falls upon them. (Eccl 9:11–12)

More often than we would like to admit, we are not as in control of our lives as we want to believe; which means that against our will we live subject to the chance of pain, disease, and loss. Just ask Job or Naomi.

Hurting with God addressed part of this struggle: learning the faith language of lament to which the Psalms testify over and over, and recognizing, as Bruggemann stated, that "all such experiences of disorder are a proper subject for discourse with God. There is nothing out of bounds, nothing precluded or inappropriate. Everything properly belongs in this conversation of the heart" (*Message of the Psalms*, 52). And yet, for reasons space does not permit us to discuss here, the church and its members have all but lost the language of lament. Once so pervasive in the Psalms, three thousand years ago, lament has become an endangered species. Consequently, when bombs detonate or fertilizer plants explode, we are at a loss for words to say to God.

We must restore lament, if for no other reason than language is the soil in which relationships grow. Soil too shallow to permit the harsh honesty and intensity of lament will never hold when the winds blow and storms let loose their vengeance—when we desperately need language and relationship with the LORD to survive the night.

After Lament

So then, what more can be said about life *After Lament*?

To begin, I find it impossible to generalize and write about life after lament as if there was a common experience we all go through. I can't do that; I can only write out of specific experiences, my own and that of others I know, including stories from the biblical text. And I need to emphasize again that this is the product of my journey—what one person is learning along the way of *Hurting with God* in lament and living with God *After Lament*.

When a person comes to a point *After Lament*, one of two things has happened: 1) God has answered the prayer "Yes," or 2) God has said "No." If the answer is "No," it might be that it is not time to give up and accept God's answer; instead, we should keep at the lament. But even then, eventually, the answer to a lament will be "Yes" or "No."

If the answer is "Yes," then call out the praise team and pull out the psalms of thanksgiving and get with it! Go back through these chapters and look for all the psalms of joy, praise, and thanksgiving that come after lament. Sing and pray these psalms. The chapters on thanksgiving, new praise, and rejoicing in the Lord were written for you. Or even better, write your own psalm of thanksgiving following the pattern we discussed in chapter five.

Most important, tell your story—for your sake and the sake of others. For your sake so that you will remember what God has done in your life and trust God in the future when the clouds move back in; for the sake of others so that the rest of us will hear testimony to God's work in the world. Even if—or especially if—God's answer to me is "No," I need to hear from you that God is still at work in the world, still doing something—even if it ticks me off that God decided to help you, but not me. How will the world come to know that there is a God, sovereign over all things, if we do not start talking about what God did when we were in desperate need? If God has done great things for us, witnessing to God's work in our lives is not optional but our responsibility. If you dared to lament, you must speak for God.

The other possible response to our lament is the answer "No." And it's my guess that, if you have come this far, you are either in a situation in which God keeps saying "No," or you are trying to minister to someone in that situation (may God bless you, even if God refuses your friend's lament). What I need to say about life after lament when God says "No" is obviously more challenging and complicated. So here goes.

Unless the lament was of little consequence (in which case what I have to say isn't really needed), life *After Lament* is at best challenging, and much of the time more difficult than anyone can imagine—other than you. Job's story can help us get started down this path. Job's situation was like and unlike typical lament. He was like many in that he never had a chance to lament for his children, to beg for their lives. By the time word reached Job, hope didn't have a chance; they were already dead and there was nothing left to do but grieve. Some of you know what that's like, and I am sorry for pain that is unimaginable to me. Job's lament was more about God's ongoing attack against his body and life in general: either kill me and get it over with or heal me and restore my life. In addition, toward the end of his speeches Job also began to charge God with being a lousy god because he was not punishing the wicked (others) and blessing the righteous (Job).

So here's my first observation, courtesy of Job. If God's answer to your lament has been "No," *beware of anyone who would dare to explain why God has caused your life such pain.* Especially beware of those who claim that it is your lack of faith or because God has some incredible plan that required your child to be born with Cerebral Palsy or for an accident to leave your spouse disabled. Job did nothing wrong, there was nothing he needed to learn, nor was there a great plan to follow. What led to Job's grief and time of lament is beyond belief—look at it: his family gets smashed because he is such a good man with faith beyond anyone else in his generation (Job 1:8). If anything is to blame, it is Job who was too good, too righteous. Job's three friends—and I use that term generously—thought it was their job to explain everything to Job: how Job must have done something wrong, how he lacked faith, or was secretly a sinner (see Job 22). And when God shows up at the end of the book, his anger is boiling over against these three fools who dared to speak for God (42:7). So let's get this straight: suffering does not come just because you did something wrong or lacked faith. If God said "No" to your prayers for a healthy child or for a safe trip for the teenagers at your church and the church van flips, when someone starts trying to explain to you that God needed another angel or that God must have some great plan that is going to come from this tragedy, don't just walk away—run! But first, you have my solemn permission to rebuke them with a holy slap across the mouth.

We'll stick with Job for a second observation. The Book of Job is not what its reputation holds it to be. What I mean is that the book is not about why people suffer or why bad things happen to good people (and good things happen to bad people). If either of these are the subject of the book, the answer is provided in the opening chapters. The reason Job suffers and God says "No" to his every lament is because God and "the Satan" make a bet (be careful not to confuse this angelic servant cast as "the attorney general" in God's heavenly court with what will later be called the Devil or Satan in the New Testament). God starts boasting about how good Job is and the Satan challenges God's evaluation, claiming that the only reason Job is so good is because God pays him so well: "Does Job serve God for nothing?" (Job 1:9). The answer, claims the Satan, is "No"—Job serves God for what Job gets out of the relationship. But if God were to stretch out his hand and "touch all that he has," Job will turn on God in a heartbeat and curse God to his face. The only reason Job or anyone serves God is for the goods they get out of the deal. Take away all the blessings from Job (or anyone) and Job will not worship God, and neither would anyone else. So the question the book raises is: *Will Job serve God for no reward?* Will Job worship God even if all he gets is pain and loss? *Will a human serve the Lord simply because the Lord is God?*

The harsh reality for those to whom God says "No" is that we face the same question Job struggles with: Will you choose to serve God anyway? Or, whatever has happened—whatever God has said "No" to— does that mean you are going to walk? It is easy to serve God and shout hallelujah as long as the payoff is there—a good life, the answer I wanted to my prayer. But what if there is no payoff, just pain? *Will you serve the Lord for absolutely no reason other than that the Lord is God?*

We move back to the Psalms for our third observation: *the action most advocated after lament by those writing laments is trust, not thanksgiving or praise.* This is closely related to our second observation, but in view of the emphasis placed on trust by the laments, I think it fair to keep trust separate from the decision to serve or worship God. We've reviewed the data from the Book of Psalms several times in our work. The sixty chapters of laments mention thanksgiving or a thank offering in only nineteen chapters, while fifty-one of these same laments urge their reader to rely on the LORD. While their circumstances are no less threatening than in other laments, these laments stand out on the basis of their confidence in the LORD to act on their behalf. In response, the Psalms answer the call for trust with at least twelve psalms that come *After Lament* and emphasize reliance on or trust in the LORD (11, 16, 18, 20, 23, 27, 41, 46, 91, 121, 125, 131): from the well-known shepherd's psalm (Ps 23), to the lesser known Psalm 131 ("I have calmed and quieted my soul, like a weaned child with its mother" [131:2]).

Trust is a prevalent theme in the laments for the simple reason that the most difficult challenge we will face during and after lament is trusting God, especially when our hopes in God come up short. So to follow the Psalms, our final observations about life *After Lament* of necessity have to do with trust. Since the Garden of Eden, our human nature has sought to control our own lives, to trust ourselves rather than the God who made us. But for those who will trust, we must first hand over control of our lives to God—or, truth be told, admit that we have never been in control of our lives. In this, those of us to whom God has said "No" have the advantage of knowing we are not in control. For me my pain is a regular reminder that I do not and cannot control my own life. Even with medication I am unable to control when and/or how severe or steady my pain will be. Whether I am sitting, standing, or lying down, I cannot predict when I may get an electrical shock that jolts me out of my socks. And just for fun, without pain, any part of my body may jerk out of control at any time. At least that's how I explain all those times my hand just happens to reach over and hit a sleeping student on the head.

When God says "No," we may also learn that our trust has been misplaced—in ourselves, other people, power, institutions, etc.—when there is only one who is in control and trustworthy. And that's the catch—learning to trust the one who sometimes disappoints, who has the power to do what we cannot do, but chooses not to do it. To believe that God is good when we receive God's gifts with thanksgiving; and that God is still good when we do not. So, it is little wonder the lament psalms lead to psalms of trust and confidence in the Lord.

Trusting the Lord doesn't mean that we believe God is directing every incidental event in our lives as part of some grand scheme that guides even God's decisions about our laments. Instead, we trust that our God will be with us and see us through whatever may happen, even if what happens is our death. Stated in different terms, to trust God is to accept what you cannot change, to accept God's answer and whatever condition or problem you asked God to remove. To help me, Dana (my wife) reminds me from time to time of the serenity prayer:

> God grant me the serenity to accept the things I
> cannot change;
> courage to change the things I can;
> and wisdom to know the difference.
>
> —Reinhold Niebuhr

As I worked through the pain management program at the Baylor University Medical Center, the first thing the clinicians pushed me to do was stop fighting my pain (which guaranteed a lost battle every day), and accept my pain as part of who I am; or welcome my pain as a house guest that I treat with hospitality. This may sound easy to do, but I can assure you, it is anything but easy. But I can also assure you that, for me, accepting God's decision has been life giving. Paul said that God told him, "My grace is sufficient for you for power is made perfect in weakness" (2 Cor 12:9). I choose to believe that God's grace is also sufficient for me—and you—and that God will be honored, not by our strength, but in our brokenness.

Remember that at the heart of our faith is a story of life out of death, and life *After Lament*. So hope that is broken and dashed is not the end of our story. We may never receive the object of our lament; but our hope is not in finding a yes to every request. Our God promises grace sufficient to our need (2 Cor 12:8–10), and nothing less than life out of death, life *After Lament*.

APPENDIX I

Works Cited

Alcott, Louisa May. *Little Women*. Roberts Brothers, 1868.

Allen, Leslie C. *Psalms 101–150*. Word Biblical Commentary. Waco, TX: Word Books, 1983.

Anderson, Bernhard, and Steven Bishop. *Out of the Depths: The Psalms Speak for Us Today*. Third Edition. Revised and Expanded. Louisville, KY: Westminster John Knox Press, 2000.

Beecher, Henry Ward. *Life Thoughts*. Boston: Phillip Sampson, 1858.

Bellinger, William H., Jr. *Psalms: A Guide to Studying the Psalter*. Second Edition. Grand Rapids, MI: Baker Academic, 2012.

Brueggemann, Walter. *The Message of the Psalms: A Theological Commentary*. Minneapolis, MN: Augsburg Fortress, 1984.

Clifford, Richard J. *Psalms 1–72* and *Psalms 73–150*. Abingdon Old Testament Commentaries. Nashville, TN: Abingdon Press, 2002 and 2003.

Craigie, Peter C. *Psalms 1–50*. Word Biblical Commentary. Waco, TX: Word Books, 1983.

Gerstenberger, Erhard. *Psalms: Part 1 with an Introduction to Cultic Poetry*, and *Psalms: Part 2, and Lamentations*. Forms of the Old Testament Literature 14 and 15. Grand Rapids, MI: William B. Eerdmans 1988 and 2001.

Grogan, Geoffrey. *Psalms*. Two Horizons Old Testament Commentary. Grand Rapids, MI: William B. Eerdmans, 2008.

Holladay, William L. *The Psalms through Three Thousand Years: Prayerbook of a Cloud of Witnesses.* Minneapolis, MN: Fortress Press, 1996.

Hopkins, Denise Dombkowski. *Journey through the Psalms.* Revised and Expanded. St. Louis, MO: Chalice, 2002.

Hossfeld, Frank-Lothar and Erich Zenger. *Psalms 2: A Commentary on Psalms 51–100* and *Psalms 3: A Commentary on Psalms 101–150.* Translated by Linda M. Maloney. Hermenia. Minneapolis, MN: Fortress Press, 2000 and 2011.

Kraus, Hans-Joachim. *Psalms 60–150.* A Continental Commentary. Translated by Hilton C. Oswald. Minneapolis, MN: Fortress Press, 1993.

Limburg, James. *Psalms.* Westminster Bible Companion. Louisville, KY: Westminster John Knox Press, 2000.

Mays, James L. *Psalms.* Interpretation. Louisville, KY: John Knox, 1994.

Miller, Patrick D. *Interpreting the Psalms.* Philadelphia, PA: Fortress Press, 1986

Murphy, Roland E. *The Gift of the Psalms.* Peabody, Mass: Hendrickson, 2000.

Pemberton, Glenn. *Hurting with God: Learning to Lament with the Psalms.* Abilene, TX: ACU Press, 2012.

Shipp, R. Mark, Ed. *Timeless: Ancient Psalms for the Church Today. Volume One: In the Day of Distress, Psalms 1–41.* Abilene, TX: ACU Press, 2011.

Tate, Marvin E. *Psalms 51–100.* Word Biblical Commentary 20. Dallas, TX: Word Books, 1990.

Terrien, Samuel. *The Psalms: Strophic Structure and Theological Commentary.* Grand Rapids, MI: William B. Eerdmans, 2003.

Westermann, Claus. *The Living Psalms.* Translated by J. R. Porter. Grand Rapids, MI: Eerdmans 1989.

Discussion Guide

Chapter One

1. Consider the stories of Job, Abraham and Isaac, and Naomi. Do you think these characters lived happily ever after? Why or why not? What other biblical characters might be considered along with these? Explain.

2. When do you think it is time to stop lamenting, asking God to change your circumstances, and accept that God has said no to your lament? What do you think about the author's claim that people of faith are prone to be in a hurry and impatient with others who do not move through lament quickly?

3. The author lists four assumptions (see p. 25) that he sees lived out by most Christians. Consider each assumption. Do you agree or disagree? Why?

4. What times of lament have you lived through? Would you say that at the end of your struggle you came back to the same place with God as before or in a different place? Explain. Did your struggle leave any scars? Explain.

Chapter Two

1. In addition to the author's comments, what do you think has caused the demise of lament?

2. Read Psalm 13 and identify each of the basic elements of lament. How do these elements work together in the psalm to create meaning and emotion?

3. Read Psalm 38 carefully. List all of the poet's complaints under the categories of physical, emotional, social, and spiritual problems. What do you make of the poet's complaints? Do you think they are literal or metaphoric?

4. Consider Liam's Lament. This prayer is similar to many psalms, but uses a contemporary situation and contemporary language. How does bringing lament up to day change the way you understand or feel about lament?

5. Write a lament about something in your life or a recent public event. Be sure to include all of the elements that are typically a part of lament. Have you ever prayed in this way? Share your lament with others in the class. See the author's laments and other prayers at https://www.facebook.com/HurtingWithGod and http://hebrewhound.wix.com/pemberton

Chapter Three

1. The author uses the image of a wagon wheel to emphasize the movement of lament; the spokes point in different directions. Can you think of other images that capture the dynamics of the laments?

2. What do you think of the psalmists who make deals with God: "If God will . . . then I will. . . ." Is this "foxhole" religion? Does it demonstrate faith or the lack of faith?

3. Have you ever experienced a time when it was difficult to sing praise or thanksgiving? Why was it difficult? What needed to happen to restore your voice?

4. The author claims that trust in the Lord is as action that may be more difficult than doing what the other spokes lead to (e.g., sing praise, give thanks). Do you agree or disagree? Why?

5. Describe a time when you have felt hopeless. What caused the hopelessness? In what ways are these causes like those in Psalm 88 and 137? In chapter 9 we will discuss these broken spokes in greater detail, but for now: what led you out of the hopelessness?

6. What does the author mean by "a fast spirituality does not equal a good spirituality"? What is the danger of a "fast spirituality"? What are some safeguards we might put in place to prevent our falling into this trap?

Chapter Four (Spoke One)

1. The author claims that trust is a difficult *action*. Do you agree or disagree? Why?

2. What are your favorite metaphors that express the psalmist's relationship to God? Which images that describe how God helps the psalmist in conflict are most encouraging to you?

3. Do you hear people say, in various ways, that there is nothing left for the righteous to do but run for safety? How does the vision of God in the temple, on his throne, help when you face trouble?

4. Is Psalm 23 one of your favorite psalms? Why or why not? What is the message of the psalm?

5. Do you think Psalm 131 was written by a woman? Why or why not? Does this make any difference to you?

6. Consider the terms *refuge, strength, and help*. Which is most encouraging to you? What does it mean to "be still and know that I am God" (46:10)? Why does the author claim that "To live in God's world takes an act of great imagination: to believe God is our refuge, our strength, and our help"? (p 87)

Chapter Five (Spoke Two)

1. Has God ever said "No" to one of your prayers? Think of one specific example. What did you pray for? What happened? How did you know that God's answer was "No"? How did you settle matters with God?

2. Has God ever said "Yes" to one of your prayers? Think of one specific example. What happened? Did the experience change you? How?

3. Write a thanksgiving psalm for what God has done in your life. Remember to include all four standard elements: an initial outburst of gratitude, a call to others to join your thanksgiving, retelling what God has done for you, and a declaration of what you will now do for God.

4. The author emphasizes that thanksgiving is a type of speech that comes in response to specific need and lament. Thus, without lament, thanksgiving has no place in our churches or our lives. Do you agree? Explain.

5. Consider the final challenge the author makes: how do we give thanks for the deliverance of one child when another dies? How can we practice authentic thanksgiving when some are still in pain?

Chapter Six (Spoke Three)

1. Have you experienced a time in your life when your praises had to be for "who God is" rather than what God was or was not doing in your life? What was happening in your life? How were you able to praise God? What role, if any, did your faith community play?

2. How might we "rejoice with those who rejoice" *and* "weep with those who weep" in our assemblies? Is it possible to do both?

3. Consider Psalms 103, 113, and 33. How are these praise psalms like other common praises? How do they differ? Do you think these psalms would be easier for a person experiencing trouble to sing? Why or why not?

4. What role does trust play in our ability to sing praises? Is it possible to sing praise without trust or with little trust? Explain. How might praise reinforce or bolster our trust?

5. What do you think of Wilson's claim about the arrangement of psalms in the Book of Psalms? If true, how might his theory impact or change the way we read or understand the psalms? For example, what might change in your reading of Psalm 23 if you realized you were to read Psalm 22 first?

6. Consider the final sentence in the chapter: "Praise, old or new, comes with sacrifice, a cost." In what sense does praise come with a cost? Explain. What costs would you say that you have paid to praise God?

Chapter Seven (Spoke Four)

1. Can you identify any enemies that will rejoice over you, if the Lord does not deliver or help you? Can you think of anyone you have helped (a lot) who, when you were in trouble, not only refused to help but took advantage of you? If so, in what ways are you able to identify with the psalmists and the requests in Psalm 35? If not, how might our lack of enemies influence our understanding of Psalm 35 and similar psalms?

2. Explain the statement: "Who rejoices in the kingdom of God is a crucial policy decision for the reign of God" (p. 138). Why is it that who the Lord decides will laugh is such an important issue? Do you agree or disagree with these claims? Why or why not?

3. Several psalms imagine nature bursting out in joy and celebration. Why is this so? What causes nature to rejoice? Do you understand these ideas as simply poetic imagery—or more literally, nature actually rejoices?

4. What do you think of the call to sing a "new song"? Why do we need new songs? What does the lack of new songs suggest about a community of faith?

5. Do you recall the last time you were overcome by joy? What happened?

6. How does joy come to the Lord's people as the result of the Lord's reign? What is it about God's reign that brings joy? Have you experienced this joy? Why or why not?

Chapter Eight (Spoke Five)

1. Do you recall singing songs of instruction? What were your favorite songs? Why? Why do you think we do not sing these songs often today?

2. What do you think is the theme of Psalm 127? Why do you think the writer thinks it necessary to tell us what is said in this psalm? Why do you think people eat "the bread of anxious toil"? What does this mean?

3. Psalm 133. Who or what do you think this psalm is talking about? How do you think unity may be achieved? The author claims that the "first challenge Psalm 133 presents is for us to become aware of just how fractured our lives have become" (p. 164). Do you agree or disagree? In what ways has your life become fractured?

4. Psalm 32. Have you ever experienced a time when you tried to hide your sin? Please describe what that time in your life was like? What caused you to confess? How did it feel to confess and receive God's forgiveness?

5. Psalm 73. Have you ever experienced a time when you were envious of the wicked? What led you to envy? What do you think happened in the sanctuary to change the psalmist's attitude? What helps you "reset" your attitude and relationship with God when your faith claims do not match your lived experience?

Chapter Nine (Spoke Six)

1. Has there ever been a time in your life that you lost hope? Please explain. Did you lose trust in God? What do you think a person can do to regain hope? What role might the faith community play?

2. Psalm 88. What do you make of God's actions in this psalm? Why has God destroyed the psalmist's hope? Do you think the psalmist has lost trust in God? Why or why not? What would you counsel the psalmist to do?

3. Psalm 39. What misconduct does the psalmist accuse God of doing? Why did he try to stay silent? What requests does the writer make? Have you ever felt like you were in the same position as this psalmist? What did you do? Is there any way to help others who feel like they must blow the whistle on God's misconduct?

4. What response or feeling do you have when you read the accusations against God in Psalm 44 and 89? Have you ever made or felt similar accusations against God? Please explain. In view of their accusations, why do you think these psalmists write/sing/pray at all?

5. Have you had "thorns" or other prayer requests denied by God? Please explain. How can we know when God's answer is no? Did God lead your life in a different direction? Make a list of how we might know when to persevere in prayer and when we should give up. Why do you think God would make us ask over and over, instead of granting our request the first time?

6. Who are those you know who have endured significant lost hopes, but continue to live by faith? What are some of the most helpful

things we may do for those who are living with lost hopes? What things may be harmful?

Chapter Ten

1. Consider how the Lord has broken your life in the past. How was your life broken? How was it rebuilt? Would you say your new life is better or was worth the pain? Why or why not?

2. Which of the chapters has been the most important for your walk with God? Why? What message or messages did you take from that chapter?

3. Share some of the *before and after* moments from your life. How have these moments defined your life? How did your life change?

4. Which of the languages that come after lament in the Psalms would you say most needs to be restored in your faith community? Why? How would the restoration of these languages help your community?

5. The author claims that in the Psalms the most important language or concern after lament is trust in God. Do you agree or disagree? Explain.

6. Identify some of the people in your faith community who are living their lives with broken hopes. What do you most admire about their faith-walk? Please take the time to write a note to these people or find and talk to them after church some day (you have no idea how much encouragement you may give them).

7. Who do you see that most needs someone to walk alongside them?

Recommended Bibliography

Short Monographs with Chapters on Psalms After Lament

Anderson, Bernhard, and Steven Bishop. *Out of the Depths: The Psalms Speak for Us Today.* Third Edition. Revised and Expanded. Louisville, KY: Westminster John Knox Press, 2000.

Bellinger, William H., Jr. *Psalms: A Guide to Studying the Psalter.* Second Edition. Grand Rapids, MI: Baker Academic, 2012.

Brueggemann, Walter. *The Message of the Psalms: A Theological Commentary.* Minneapolis, MN: Augsburg Fortress, 1984.

Hopkins, Denise Dombkowski. *Journey through the Psalms.* Revised and Expanded. St. Louis, MO: Chalice, 2002.

Mays, James L. *The Lord Reigns: A Theological Handbook to the Psalms.* Louisville, KY: Westminster John Knox Press, 1994.

Miller, Patrick D. *Interpreting the Psalms.* Philadelphia, PA: Fortress Press, 1986

Murphy, Roland E. *The Gift of the Psalms.* Peabody, Mass: Hendrickson, 2000.

Concise Commentaries Especially Helpful for Teaching the Psalms

Clifford, Richard J. *Psalms 1–72* and *Psalms 73–150*. Abingdon Old Testament Commentaries. Nashville, TN: Abingdon Press, 2002 and 2003.

Limburg, James. *Psalms*. Westminster Bible Companion. Louisville, KY: Westminster John Knox Press, 2000.

Mays, James L. *Psalms*. Interpretation. Louisville, KY: John Knox, 1994.

Preaching the Psalms

Bland, Dave, and David Fleer, Eds. *Performing the Psalms*. St. Louis, MO: Chalice, 2005.

Chisholm, Bob, and Dave Bland, Eds. *An Honest Cry: Sermons from the Psalms in Honor of Prentice A. Meador Jr.* Abilene, TX: Leafwood, 2010.

Mays, James L. *Preaching and Teaching the Psalms*. Edited by Patrick Miller and Gene Tucker. Louisville, KY: Westminster John Knox Press, 2006.

Other Recommended Works

Brueggemann, Walter. *The Psalms and the Life of Faith*. Patrick D. Miller, Ed. Minneapolis, MN: Fortress, 1995.

Brown, William P. *Seeing the Psalms: A Theology of Metaphor*. Louisville, KY: Westminster John Knox Press, 2002.

Jacobson, Rolf A., Ed. *Soundings in the Theology of Psalms: Perspectives and Methods in Contemporary Scholarship*. Minneapolis, MN: Fortress, 2011.

Johnston, Philip S., and David G. Firth. *Interpreting the Psalms: Issues and Approaches*. Downers Grove, Il: InterVarsity Press, 2005.

McCann, J. Clinton Jr., and James C. Howell. *Preaching the Psalms*. Nashville, TN: Abingdon, 2001.

Reid Stephen Breck, Ed. *Psalms and Practice. Worship, Virtue, and Authority*. Collegeville, MI: Liturgical Press, 2001.

Wenham, Gordon J. *Psalms as Torah: Reading Biblical Song Ethically*. Grand Rapids, MI: Baker, 2012.

Technical Studies and Commentaries

Allen, Leslie C. *Psalms 101–150*. Word Biblical Commentary. Waco, TX: Word Books, 1983.

Craigie, Peter C. *Psalms 1–50*. Word Biblical Commentary. Waco, TX: Word Books, 1983.

Gunkel, Hermann. *An Introduction to the Psalms: The Genres of the Religious Lyric of Israel*. Translated by James D. Nogalski. Macon, GA: Mercer University Press, 1998.

Hossfeld, Frank-Lothar and Erich Zenger. *Psalms 2: A Commentary on Psalms 51–100* and *Psalms 3: A Commentary on Psalms 101–150*. Translated by Linda M. Maloney. Hermenia. Minneapolis, MN: Fortress Press, 2000 and 2011.

Kraus, Hans-Joachim. *Psalms 1–59* and *Psalms 60–150*. A Continental Commentary. Translated by Hilton C. Oswald. Minneapolis, MN: Fortress Press, 1993.

McCann, J. Clinton Jr., Ed. *Shape and Shaping of the Psalter*. JSOTSup 159. Sheffield: JSOT Press, 1993.

Mowinckel, Sigmund. *The Psalms in Israel's Worship*. Translated by D. R. Ap-Thomas. Grand Rapids, MI: William B. Eerdmans, 2004.

Tate, Marvin E. *Psalms 51–100*. Word Biblical Commentary 20. Dallas, TX: Word Books, 1990.

Terrien, Samuel. *The Psalms: Strophic Structure and Theological Commentary*. Grand Rapids, MI: William B. Eerdmans, 2003.

DeClaisse-Walford, Nancy L. *Reading From The Beginning: The Shaping of the Hebrew Psalter*. Macon, GA: Mercer University Press, 1997.

Westermann, Claus. *Praise and Lament in the Psalms*. Atlanta, GA: John Knox, 1981.

Wilson, Gerald Henry. *The Editing of the Hebrew Psalter*. SBLDiss 76. Chico, CA: Scholar's Press, 1985.

Index to Psalms
in *After Lament*